experience and a passion for travel.

Rely on Thomas Cook as your travelling companion on your next trip and benefit from our unique heritage.

Thomas Cook **pocket** guides

KIEV

Tom Burgess

Your travelling companion since 1873

Thomas Cook

Written by Tom Burgess, updated by Debbie Stowe

Published by Thomas Cook Publishing
A division of Thomas Cook Tour Operations Limited
Company registration no. 3772199 England
The Thomas Cook Business Park, Unit 9, Coningsby Road,
Peterborough PE3 8SB, United Kingdom
Email: books@thomascook.com, Tel: +44 (0) 1733 416477
www.thomascookpublishing.com

Produced by Cambridge Publishing Management Limited
Burr Elm Court, Main Street, Caldecote CB23 7NU
www.cambridgepm.co.uk

ISBN: 978-1-84848-503-7

Series Editor: Karen Beaulah
Production/DTP: Steven Collins

Printed and bound in Spain by GraphyCems

CONTENTS

SYMBOLS KEY

The following symbols are used throughout this book:

address telephone website address email
opening times public transport connections important

The following symbols are used on the maps:

airport
hospital
police station
bus station
railway station
metro
cathedral
1 numbers denote featured cafés & restaurants

point of interest
city
large town
small town
main road
minor road
railway
international border

Hotels and restaurants are graded by approximate price as follows:
£ budget price **££** mid-range price **£££** expensive **££££** very expensive

The following abbreviations are used for addresses:

bul. *bulvar* (boulevard)
pl. *ploscha* (square)
prosp. *prospekt* (avenue)
prov. *provulok* (lane, minor street)
vul. *vulytsia* (street)

Opening hours are daily unless specified otherwise.

A mix of modern and neoclassical styles in the city suburbs

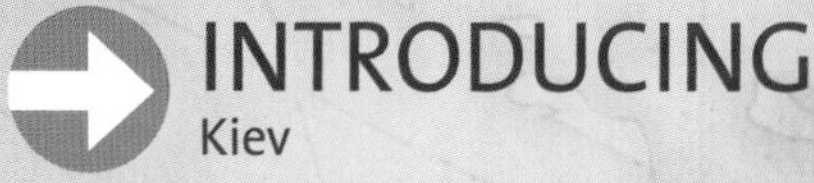

INTRODUCING
Kiev

Introduction

Visit Kiev, capital of Ukraine, and you'll notice a vibrancy about the place. There's a special buzz in the streets, bars and restaurants that's hard to ignore. Youth, enthusiasm and massive recent investment, albeit tempered by the global economic downturn of the late 2000s, are all playing a vital role in Kiev's reassertion of itself as one of Europe's most culturally important and sophisticated cities.

Kiev's colourful history stretches back thousands of years, from Viking invasions in the 9th century and the establishment of Orthodox Christianity as the official religion in the 10th century to Ukraine's more recent struggles for independence from Russian and Soviet rule. There are plenty of mementoes of the distant and not-so-distant past dotted about the city. The beautiful Byzantine St Sophia's Cathedral, for instance, is about a millennium old and the ancient Caves Monastery draws visitors from all over the world. You'll see statues to both Yaroslav the Wise and Lenin (the latter having been restored after its nose and hand were smashed in a 2009 attack by political activists). These monuments and reminders

Kiev rushes ahead with its progressive makeover

of the past co-exist with symbols of 21st-century sophistication, such as the modern airport and rail terminals.

You'll still find some hangovers from the communist era, such as the drab, nondescript tenement blocks that characterise the suburbs, but these are quickly being caught up in an extensive urban makeover and restoration project that's fanning outward from the centre and gradually changing the city's appearance. Chief among these projects is Ukraine's hosting of the Euro 2012 tournament, which has brought in huge investment in facilities and infrastructure.

Tourism is picking up as word gets out that Kiev is the latest hot destination, whether for a short weekend break or a longer stay. Cultural events and performances fill theatres and concert halls, while family-run shops and bustling markets make a change from the usual European brands. Food is tasty and novel, and the weather, in spring and summer at least, is perfect. Add to this the warm hospitality of the Ukrainian people and the affordable cost of living and holidaying in the city, and you'll be glad you arrived here before the crowds.

KIEV OR KYIV?

The city is still best known in the English-speaking world as Kiev, a spelling that dates back to when Ukraine (no longer 'The Ukraine') was part of the Russian Empire and the Soviet Union. Due to its familiarity, that is the name used throughout this book. The correct transliteration, however, is 'Kyiv', and this version is coming into increasing use in the West. As it is closer to the Ukrainian name and has no association with the days of Russian domination, this is the Romanised spelling that Ukrainians prefer; but if you say 'Kiev' and they say 'Kyiv', no one's going to suggest calling the whole thing off.

When to go

SEASONS & CLIMATE

Far from the year-round frozen wasteland that many envisage, Kiev has four distinct seasons. Although the winter can be harsh, the other three seasons are at least pleasant, and summer temperatures can reach 35°C (95°F). Any period from the beginning of May to the middle of October is a good time to visit. The weather then is warm to hot, with plenty of sunshine, the fields and trees are green, and the markets are full of fresh fruits and vegetables.

Spring and autumn are generally quite short, although warm and mild. Perhaps the very best month is May, when the sun begins to shine in earnest, and the flowers and trees start to bloom and put on their finest greenery. This is the month the citizens of Kiev like the best, and it is the time when the city begins to come alive

after the winter. Harvest time is in October, when the fields around Kiev are at their most picturesque. Summer is generally hot, with long days and lots of sunshine. Many of the most colourful cultural festivals occur in summer, and the tourist facilities are open, so it is a good time to visit. It does get very hot in July and August, but thankfully almost all hotels, restaurants and other buildings have air conditioning.

Winters are not as cold as they used to be; November nights can be frosty but winter doesn't start properly until the middle of December, when temperatures drop below freezing during both day and night. The snow generally begins to thaw at the end of February and spring arrives in the middle of March, although there can still be occasional snow showers in April and early May.

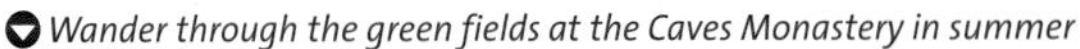

Wander through the green fields at the Caves Monastery in summer

ANNUAL EVENTS

Many music and film festivals occur during the year in Kiev. The biggest challenge is locating up-to-date information on these events before your visit. The following are the best publicised.

January

Gregorian New Year (1 January) Though less of a knees-up than the Julian version, few are churlish enough to ignore the excuse for a party.

Golden icon in the Saint Sophia Orthodox Cathedral

Orthodox Christmas (6 & 7 January) This is Ukraine's Christmas proper, with festive anticipation on the eve preparing the way for celebrations (some less pious than others) on the big day.
Julian New Year (14 January) Survivors of the pan-denominational Chrimbo look resolutely to the future.
Orthodox Epiphany (19 January) Kiev's hardiest souls leap into the River Dnipro to celebrate the arrival of Christ. And that's orthodox?

March

International Women's Day (8 March) Gifts and flowers are given to women of all ages. This is not a day when sisters are doing it for themselves, however, as men do the cooking and cleaning for the women in their life.

April

Orthodox Easter (15 April 2012; 5 May 2013; 20 April 2014) This is the most important religious holiday in Ukraine, with long church services, other rituals and public displays. Special foods and elaborately decorated Easter eggs are prepared for blessing by the priests.

May

Labour Day/May Day (1 & 2 May) Despite the event being a hangover from the Soviet era, the contribution made by the working person is zealously celebrated.
Victory Day (9 May) This festival celebrates the Soviet Union's victory over the Nazis in World War II with spectacular firework displays.
Days of the Capital (last weekend in May) This is the city's biggest and best street festival, drawing up to 50,000 visitors to partake of food, music and merriment in the capital, centred on the Andrew's

Descent area. This is a time when Kiev really kicks up its heels and celebrates its heritage.

End May–beginning June

Kiev International Film Festival A celebration of Ukrainian culture and cinema in general, this competitive event showcases both local and world titles. Ⓦ www.kievfilmfest.com

Summer

Global East Rock Festival After being established in 2009, this open-air rock and metal extravaganza has now gone international, with a Georgian version being held in 2011. The precise timing and the venue vary, so rockers should consult the website for more details. Ⓦ www.globaleastfan.com

July

Ivan Kupala (St John's Baptism) (7 July) This originated as a pagan ritual in honour of summer, but mutated into a Christian holiday with the arrival of Orthodoxy. Its main objectives are spiritual cleansing through the judicious application of fire and water.

August

Ukrainian Independence Day (24 August) This is the summer's big one, held to celebrate the split from the Soviet Union in 1991. Mammoth parades and long-winded political speeches are its hallmarks.

October

Kiev International Film Festival – Molodist (late October) This international festival for young and first-time filmmakers has been taking place since 1970 and draws high-profile names such as Roman Polanski and Jerzy Hoffman as guest speakers. W www.molodist.com

December

Catholic Christmas (25 December) Ukrainians of all religious backgrounds need no persuading to whoop it up as the annual Christmas fest kicks off.

PUBLIC HOLIDAYS

New Year's Day 1 Jan
Orthodox Christmas Day 7 Jan
International Women's Day 8 Mar
Orthodox Easter 15 Apr 2012; 5 May 2013; 20 April 2014
Labour Day/May Day 1 & 2 May
Victory Day 9 May
Holy Trinity Day 4 June 2012; 24 June 2013; 9 June 2014
Constitution Day 28 June
Ukrainian Independence Day 24 Aug

As there is a rule to compensate holiday Sundays by prolonging the weekend to Monday, people do not work on the Mondays immediately after Easter, Holy Trinity Day or any of the listed public holidays if they coincide with Sundays.

Urban legends

It is not just tales of Baba Yaga the sorceress, a central figure in Ukrainian children's stories, or yarns about brave Cossack warriors that permeate the local folklore. For some reason, Kiev's city landmarks have accumulated a set of urban legends that are a joy because they don't even try to be credible. Here are just a few.

The Bald Mountain of Vydubychi

Most bald peaks in folklore are thought to have been the result of pagans cutting down all the trees in that area to build a temple, and in Christian times bald mountains frequently came to be considered places of evil. The Bald Mountain of Vydubychi has a long history that stretches back to the time of the warrior Batu Khan. After capturing Kiev he ordered the deaths of all the residents. The Kyivans fled to the caves of Zverynts and Kitayev; enraged, Batu Khan had the entrances to the caves bricked up. It is said that the restless souls of those who died still wander there. At the end of the 19th century a fort was built on the site and it was later used as a place of execution. All in all the Bald Mountain of Vydubychi has not been a happy place. Metro: Vydubychi

Diakova's Disturbance

The building in question is one of the wings of the present-day Central Post Office. It was once inhabited by a rather eccentric woman known as Diakova. During the 1950s the city's newspapers carried a sensational story claiming that cushions, blankets and bed sheets had been observed flying around her bedroom. At the same time the furniture began to move and the floors to creak. Lest you think that these were merely the delusions of an ageing crackpot, they were observed by members of the local constabulary. The police, bewildered by what they had seen, sealed the apartment and relocated Diakova to a new home. Nobody uttered the word 'poltergeist' at the time, and the weird goings-on were eventually documented as an 'anomaly'. It is possibly the first recorded experience of poltergeist activity in Europe. ⓐ Khreschatyk 22 Ⓜ Metro: Maidan Nezalezhnosti

House with Chimeras

You won't have trouble identifying this house, one of the weirdest buildings in Kiev. The façade is decorated with fantastic sculptures of chimeras and animals that look more like gargoyles than anything found in nature. Concrete heads of elephants, crocodiles, rhinoceros and antelope line the walls; elephants' trunks are used as gutters and sea monsters form the roof. Legend has it that renowned Ukrainian architect Vladyslav Horodetsky built the house in memory of a daughter who had drowned in the River Dnipro – hence the sculptures evoking the underwater kingdom. The truth is, however, that he had a passion for hunting and drew inspiration from the animals he saw (and shot) in Africa. The house is now used as a reception palace by Ukraine's president and you can only enter by invitation. ⓐ Bankova 10 Ⓜ Metro: Khreschatyk

Richard's Castle

There is a local belief that this 'medieval castle' once played host to Richard the Lionheart on his return from a crusade. However, the building didn't appear until 1904. Dmitriy Orlov, a local contractor, wanted to build a house in the English neo-Gothic style: when it was completed it was an astonishing sight, with pointed spires, battlements, a covered staircase and a wonderfully romantic English garden. But it was 700 years too late to be a stopping place for King Dick. ⓐ Andriivsky uzviz 15 Ⓜ Metro: Kontraktova Ploscha

History

Simply by virtue of its location, Kiev knows a great deal about the pros and cons of being important. The degree of this importance, and the fact that many powerful nations have wanted a piece of the commercial and strategic action its location promises, have given the city a wildly turbulent history. Take, for example, the effect of the Vikings' interest.

The Norsemen took control of the city in the middle of the 9th century, when an expedition to secure an overland trade route from the north to Constantinople awoke them to the city's tremendous military and commercial potential. They were not alone in this: Prince Oleg, ruler of Novgorod, promptly wiped the Viking princes out and formed a vast empire that ran from the Baltic to Moldavia, with Kiev as its capital.

Nearly 400 years of stability were, however, crucial to the city's development. Written laws were set down, and in 988 Orthodox Christianity was established as the official religion. But in 1240, Mongols under Batu Khan (Genghis' grandson) captured and virtually destroyed the city. In 1362 it was annexed to the Lithuanian principality, and a minor renaissance was obliterated in 1482 when the Mongols destroyed the city once again.

In 1569 Kiev came under Polish control, and it was at this time that the country got its name, 'U-krayi-na' (meaning 'borderland', or, rather aptly, 'on the edge'). This period also saw the rise of the Cossacks. These were local farmers who became de facto warriors in order to defend their homes and farms against attack. In 1654 they drove the Poles out of Kiev under the leadership of Bohdan Khmelnytsky, but were forced to form an alliance with Russia that brought them under Russian jurisdiction. Any real hopes of Ukrainian independence were dashed in 1709, when Tsar Peter I took complete control of Ukraine; but he at least recast Kiev as a major city, and, under 200 years of Tsarist rule, the place regenerated and became a thriving centre once more.

The curse of being just too damned attractive struck again in the early 20th century, and Kiev entered a desperate period. During the Russian Revolution and the civil wars that ran from 1917 to 1921, the city changed hands no fewer than 18 times as the Ukrainians fought unsuccessfully to free themselves from Soviet rule. Both Lenin and Stalin wrought havoc on Ukraine, with famines, purges and genocide. More death and destruction befell Kiev when the Nazis captured the city in June 1941. By the time the Russians recaptured it in 1943, half of its population, including almost all of its Jewish community, had been killed. After the war, though, the Soviet Union started to rebuild the city. All it needed now was to be free.

As so often in history, a calamity presented an opportunity: the Chernobyl disaster in 1986 triggered a push for freedom and, with the collapse of the Soviet Union, Ukraine finally declared independence on 24 August 1991.

Since 1991, Ukraine's development has been fairly steady but marred at times by economic and political uncertainty. The Orange Revolution of November 2004 saw peaceful protests against corruption nationwide, while elections were frequently rendered meaningless by accusations of vote-rigging. In May 2008 Ukraine finally became a member of the World Trade Organisation – just before the global economic crisis hit in the second half of the year. Exchange rates plunged and the economy took a nosedive. Ukrainians are used to turbulent times, however, and as the country slowly recovers from the crisis, thoughts are turning to a happier event for the city – its Olympic Stadium is due to host the Euro 2012 football final.

Lifestyle

Kiev is striving hard to be the most prosperous and developed city in the country, and an ever-evolving skyline is a testament to the improvements taking place. The global economic downtown in 2008 revealed the true state of the economy, however – that of a country still learning to confront poverty. Flashy, fashion-filled shopping centres are surrounded by old women trying to make ends meet by selling vegetables or prized possessions. High-end Mercedes and SUVs with tinted windows career past pedestrians waiting patiently for public transport. In Kiev these early days of the new republic present economic challenges that are fascinating to observe and describe but not always fun to live with.

The early years of independence were economically harsh for most residents. Because so many people had either laboured in government factories producing overpriced goods, or been members of the military, they saw their employment simply disappear with the creation of a new nation. Those who did remain employed often went several months without receiving any pay. In addition, high inflation destroyed any pensions or savings that older people had. Despite the difficulties, they survived, thanks in no small part to the tenacious Ukrainian spirit.

If tenacity defines the Ukrainian personality, then it is family that defines the Ukrainian soul. The family network goes way beyond the immediate family and incorporates aunts, uncles and cousins – dozens of cousins. Grandparents quite frequently are the ones who care for the children, and in turn young adults care for the elderly. Ukrainians are very hospitable people and keen to engage in discussion with foreigners. Don't be surprised to be invited to their home, if only for a cup of tea (see page 21).

Central city living in Kiev's colourful houses and apartments

No matter what economic conditions prevail, the residents of Kiev always manage to keep their urban style. Even if they can't afford the luxuries of life, there is still an appreciation of the finer things. Ukrainians always wear their best clothes and shoes in public, no matter how dire their circumstances. The Western impulse to dress casually when travelling is a difficult concept for most Kiev citizens

Relaxing with a drink is as much a part of life in Kiev as in Western cities

ETIQUETTE

Ukrainians are a warm and hospitable people, and it's far from inconceivable that a timid request for directions, say, could result in your being invited to somebody's home. If you are, it is traditional to take a gift. The days when turning up with a pair of jeans gift-wrapped in newspaper would guarantee you the run of the house are gone; a bottle of wine, a toy for the children, a cake or some flowers are always appropriate (though if you choose the latter, make sure you bring an odd number of blooms: even numbers are reserved for funerals).

Be ready to accept all food and drink that's offered – refusing is considered rude. Expect to receive a toast and be prepared to extend one in return. Make it flowery and long: mumbling 'cheers' or 'all the best' or making the peace sign in response just won't do.

When visiting a church, women should keep their heads covered, and men should remove their hats.

If you are attending a business meeting, your dress and deportment should be conservative.

to comprehend, so make an effort to dress nicely and you'll find your reception more positive. After all, to Kyivans, if you are wealthy enough to travel to Kiev, surely you must be able to dress well.

Cultural life is also strong in the city. Folk dancing remains popular at weddings and festivals, and handicrafts are an everyday part of life. As for music, Ukrainians sing when they are happy and sing when they are sad. Prepare to be fascinated by the merging of independence with old traditions.

Culture

Kiev has long been culturally significant: once a city has been the focal point for the spread of Christianity throughout Eastern Europe, it's a doddle to synthesise a few disparate influences into a coherent identity.

The city knows its arias from its Elvis. You'll find an astonishing cultural range here, including such great venues as the Taras Shevchenko National Opera and Ballet Theatre, the National Philharmonic for classical music, the Palace of Sport for rock and pop and the **Ukraine National Palace of Arts** (ⓐ Chervonoarmiyska (Velyka Vasylkivska) 103 ⓣ 247 2316 Metro: Palats "Ukrayina").

Live theatre is very popular, but almost all the productions are in Ukrainian or Russian. A better option may be a ballet or classical opera performance; the latter are conducted in the original language.

Indigenous music is derived almost exclusively from the folk tradition of storytelling, in Ukraine's case through the epic poems known collectively as *dumy* that were transmitted across the country by wandering minstrels known as *kobzari*. Mincing from town to town plucking one's *kobza* (lute) and singing patriotic ditties might seem like a cushy little number, but it wasn't all supple song and dreamy lullabies: for a start, a *kobzar* was really expected to be blind; and then there were the chords – the *kobza* was in time replaced by the *bandura*, a larger instrument that could have up to 65 strings! Today the *bandura* is regarded as Ukraine's national instrument, and you can hear performances of music composed for it at the National Philharmonic and many other venues. Thanks to composer Mykola Lysenko, a more sophisticated variety of Ukrainian music has wedded the traditions of folk to piano-based classical music, and this has evolved into 'national music'.

Taras Shevchenko, the father of Ukrainian literature, is honoured all over Kiev

Ukrainian folk dancing is either Cossack or Hutsul. The Cossack dancers are known for their twirls, leaps and signature duck-kick. By contrast, the Hutsul dancers perform more of a foot-stomping choreography. Either version will leave you breathless from simply watching the high-energy performances.

Kiev has certainly had its share of struggling artists and few have crossed into the Western art realm, possibly because classical romantic painting did not feature as strongly in Ukraine as in other parts of the world. The exceptions to this are Ilya Repin and Ivan Aivazovsky, whose works are displayed worldwide.

Hand-painted Easter eggs are typical of Ukrainian craftwork

Arts and crafts provide another important facet of cultural life in Ukraine. The quintessential Ukrainian handcraft is the decoration of *pysanky*, or Easter eggs. Elaborate geometric designs cover the eggs, with flowers and animals as popular motifs, though the designs vary greatly from region to region. Other crafts include carving small wooden boxes, painting stove tiles and *rushnyky* (embroidered hand-towels that are used for special occasions such as christenings, weddings, holiday meals and funerals).

With a literacy rate of 98 per cent, it shouldn't come as any surprise that the written word plays an important part in cultural life. Taras Shevchenko (see page 26) is considered both a poet laureate and national hero. Other writers whose work has been translated for consumption in the West include Lesya Ukrainka and Mykola Hohol (Nikolai Gogol), the latter being a prominent Russian writer of Ukrainian origin who penned *The Government Inspector* and *Dead Souls*. Ukrainians can also lay claim to works by Pushkin and Chekhov, who wrote in Russian but lived in the country for part of their lives. Owning books is something of a status symbol and people are very possessive of their small personal libraries. A gift of a good book is always welcome.

Not all culture in Kiev is classical or traditional. Pop culture is making serious inroads into society, and Ukrainian pop itself mixes folk tunes with modern beats; techno music here has a distinct polka rhythm, and if that doesn't have you rushing to book your flight, nothing will.

Even more popular than a night at the ballet or symphony is a night spent at the cinema. Going to a movie in Kiev requires that you not only buy a ticket, but book a particular seat. For cinemas showing films in their original language, see page 89.

TARAS SHEVCHENKO

Most would say that this man was Ukraine's Shakespeare; if you're not a close student of his work before you come to Kiev, there's at least no danger that you'll still think he played for Chelsea by the time you leave.

Taras Hryhorovych Shevchenko is a national hero in Ukraine, and was – is – a massive influence on its language, culture and identity. Perhaps his genius was forged in adversity, for the boy Taras had it tough. Born in 1814 to a peasant family, he was orphaned as a youth but somehow gained an education in St Petersburg, where he studied painting. In 1840, he published his first collection of poems, *Kobzar*, to great acclaim.

An early revolutionary thinker, Shevchenko unsurprisingly championed the causes of the peasants of Ukraine, Ukrainian independence and the Ukrainian language, which he used extensively in his writings. Indeed this was his greatest cultural contribution: his use of Ukrainian, rather than Russian, combined with his eloquence in it, elevated the language to a universally accepted form of expression in his native country. Shevchenko was rather too much of a man of the people for Tsar Nicholas, and he was eventually imprisoned and exiled. He did regain a freedom of sorts, but his experiences had wrecked his health, and he died in 1861 at the age of 47. But by then the work of this part-Woody Guthrie, part-Virgil, part-Vera Lynn had caught the imagination of the Ukrainian people. It has never let go.

More than one monument portrays the siblings (see page 74) who founded Kiev

MAKING THE MOST OF
Kiev

Shopping

When shopping in Kiev, be prepared for the fact that everyone, from the shop attendants to the street vendors, will only allow you to purchase what they deem is best for you. The attitude is definitely different from Western shopping, but this gentle interference is done with the best of intentions. The street vendor only wants you to have the freshest product, not necessarily the one you picked – so she will exchange it for you. The well-dressed shop assistants know their fashions and if something doesn't do you justice, they won't hesitate to let you know, or refuse to let you buy it! It is okay to be choosy; it shows good taste on your part. Just make sure you remember to be polite.

Shops in Kiev normally open at 10.00 and nowadays do not close for lunch, staying open until 20.00 or, in the case of larger shops, 22.00. Since independence, the city has been transformed from a place where it was difficult to buy anything to a place where you can buy almost everything.

If you want to shop with the rich and famous, head for the underground Globus Shopping Centre at Maidan Nezalezhnosti (Independence Square). This is one of the largest of Kiev's shopping centres, with two floors laden with glitz and glamour. Fashionistas also head to Mandarin Plaza (see page 82) for the most up-to-the-minute offerings.

Kiev is already beginning to show signs of globalised capitalism, with mobile-phone dealers and designer outlets everywhere. TsUM, the old Soviet-era department store at the intersection of Khreschatyk and Bohdana Khmelnytskoho, is referred to by the locals as the Harrods of Kiev. Don't worry though – it offers a whole range of affordable goods, so you can go to buy rather than simply browse.

Vyshyvanky – *traditional embroidered shirts – make perfect souvenirs*

Are you ready to shop where the locals do? Head to one of the open markets close to Kontraktova ploscha or Lybidska metro stations, where you'll find piles of merchandise from Italy and Turkey. Be prepared to bargain.

If souvenirs are what you seek, you'll find no lack of shops along Khreschatyk filled with *matryoshkas* (what we call Russian dolls), *shapkas* (fur hats) and *rushnyky* (embroidered towels). Some other traditional Ukrainian gifts include brightly painted woodenware, charcoal-fired black pottery, and jewellery made from amber. The best souvenir market in the city is on Andriivsky uzviz (Andrew's

BABUSHKAS

You will see many older women in traditional dark plain clothing and with covered heads on the streets selling small items such as apples and shoelaces. Their plight is tragic, but their resolve is strong. As younger women, they were often left on their own for long periods of time as the menfolk were off doing military or other Soviet service. This made these women strong and independent. They were entitled to decent pensions under the old Soviet system; however, with independence, followed by massive inflation, their pensions and what little savings they had disappeared. Most are now penniless and depend on family members for food and shelter. Their strength and independent resolve drive them into the streets to do manual labour, or to sell small items to make a little money to help out at home. Do not hesitate to buy from these women, and if you give them a little extra, you will get a smile that could melt an iceberg.

USEFUL SHOPPING PHRASES

What time do the shops open/close?
О котрій відчиняються/зачиняються магазини?
O kotriy vidchyniayut'sia/zachyniayut'sia mahazyny?

How much is this?
Скільки це коштує?
Skilky tse koshtuye?

What size is this?
Який це розмір?
Yakyi tse rozmir?

Can I try this on?
Чи можу я це приміряти?
Chy mozhu ya tse prymiriaty?

My size is . . .
Мій розмір . . .
Miy rozmir . . .

I'll take this one, thank you
Я візьму це, дякую
Ya viz'mu tse, diakuyu

Can you show me the one in the window/this one?
Ви можете показати мені те що на вітрині/оце?
Vy mozhete pokazaty meni te scho na vitryni/otse?

Descent). The street is always packed with tourists, but be careful – not everything you see is the real deal.

You'll be disappointed if you come to Kiev hoping to buy some authentic Soviet paraphernalia, as it's mostly all gone. Today, anything with a red star emblazoned upon it has most likely been produced in China.

Eating & drinking

There are two staples to the Ukrainian diet: bread and *borsch*. Both come from the fertile lands that make up the country.

Ukraine has long been known as the breadbasket of Europe, and bread is central to the local culture. There is a traditional 'Bread and Salt' ceremony to welcome guests of honour, and the cry of 'Bread, Peace and Land' was used to rally the citizens during the Russian Revolution. The traditional bread is black, and made from rye flour and buckwheat. Visitors may not find it all that palatable, but other varieties, such as sourdough and white bread, are readily available. Bread is normally eaten with salads and soups.

Borsch, often mistakenly referred to as beetroot soup, starts with a vegetable or meat stock, to which is added cabbage, potato and onion. Beetroot is added to give colour and flavour. Other vegetables may be included, as are herbs such as dill. There is no set recipe, and the final product depends upon the cook and on what vegetables are available at the time of cooking. In many homes, especially among those of the not-so-well-off, *borsch* is made in large quantities and may be served three times a day. Good *borsch* has a tangy flavour, and should be so thick that a spoon does not sink into it. *Borsch* is traditionally eaten with *pampushkas* – small, round pieces of white

Borsch *is more than a humble beetroot soup*

bread flavoured with garlic. If ordered in a restaurant, it will usually be served with bread and thick cream.

Other local foods include *varenyky* – dumplings stuffed with meat, cheese or potato – and *holubtsi* – a mixture of rice and meat rolled up in cabbage leaves and served with a tomato sauce. Meat is still considered luxury food in Ukraine, and when available, pork is preferred to beef. Fish and chicken are also popular. Chicken Kiev did originate here, but you will find it only on restaurant menus.

Ukrainians have a sweet tooth. Traditional sweets, usually wrapped in bright-coloured paper, can be purchased from shops, street vendors and restaurants; the best combine honey, nuts and chocolate. Ice cream is another favourite in Kiev, and it is eaten year-round – even in the dead of winter.

Kiev's restaurants are quickly becoming very cosmopolitan, so if you do not like, or have had enough of, the local cuisine, you will have no problem finding food from just about any other part of the world. Fast-food restaurants are growing in number, so it is easy to find burgers and pizza. Most of the better establishments have menus in English, and a member of staff who speaks it. When ordering, make sure you understand the pricing structure of the restaurant you are in. In many cases there are 'extras'; these can include bread and condiments. Also, some places charge by weight (usually per

PRICE CATEGORIES

The restaurant price guides used in this book indicate the approximate cost of a three-course meal for one person, excluding drinks, at the time of writing.

£ up to 60hr. **££** 60–120hr. **£££** 120–180hr. **££££** over 180hr.

A peaceful park setting for a coffee

USEFUL DINING PHRASES

I would like a table for . . . people
Я хочу замовити столик на . . . осіб
Ya hochu zamovyty stolyk na . . . osib

Excuse me, please may we order?
Вибачте, ми можемо зробити замовлення?
Vybachte, my mozhemo zrobyty zamovlennia?

Do you have any vegetarian dishes?
Чи є у вас вегетаріанські страви?
Chy ye u vas vehetarians'ki stravy?

Where is the toilet (restroom), please?
Де знаходиться туалет?
De znahodytsia tualet?

May I have the bill, please?
Я можу отримати рахунок?
Ya mozhu otrymaty rakhunok?

100 grams), rather than portion, so be sure you know whether this is the case before you 'supersize' your order.

Breakfast does not seem to be in the Ukrainian lexicon, as Ukrainians tend to eat the same food for all three daily meals. Not to worry: most hotels serve a Western European-style buffet breakfast that includes breads, pastries, cereals, meats, cheeses and fresh fruit.

The national drink – if not the national pastime – in Ukraine is vodka, or *horilka* in Ukrainian. It is readily available in stores, and many rural families brew their own. The consumption of vodka is so high and so widespread that alcoholism is a major problem. Any excuse seems a good reason for a 'toast', and refusal of a drink when offered may be considered rude. Warning: do not try to match a Ukrainian drink for drink, and stick to known brand names. Home-made and bootleg vodka are common, and some can cause serious illness, or even death.

Other alcoholic beverages, such as beer and wine, are also readily available, but most of it is produced locally, including famous European brands such as Stella Artois and Staropramen. You can find imported beer and wine at upmarket restaurants and shops.

Coffee and tea are served everywhere, but you must ask for cream or milk to be added if you want them. Fruit juices produced from locally grown fruit are common, but many are an acquired taste. Mineral water, both Ukrainian and imported, is easily obtained.

Tipping is not traditional in Ukraine, but is becoming more common, especially in Kiev. A tip of 10–15 per cent is recommended, especially in more upmarket restaurants and bars. Some restaurants are starting to add a 5–10 per cent service charge, so read the bill carefully when it arrives.

Entertainment & nightlife

Like most things in Kiev, the nightlife is a mix of the good, the bad and the weird. The city has an abundant mix of pubs and lounges, most of which are the haunts of foreigners and Kiev's *nouveaux riches*. Because of the cost of alcohol, you'll quickly discover that most locals will buy a beer on the street and do their socialising outside when the weather permits. Wisely, the city closes the main street of Khreschatyk to vehicle traffic on weekends and holidays, so you'll only have to watch out for lurching pedestrians as opposed to a Lada being driven erratically.

Kiev's nightlife is second to none – if you enjoy all things bold and brash. Striptease is considered to be a classy addition to a club, venues are often open until the early hours, and the most recent craze is *dyscoteky*. The discos and dance clubs are a truly eclectic mix, as each new venue strives hard to outdo the other in lavishness – such as the trendy **Arena Entertainment** (ⓐ Baseina 2A ⓣ 492 0000 ⓦ www.arena-kiev.com ⓛ 22.00–06.00 Tues–Sun ⓝ Metro: Ploscha Lva Tolstoho) or the **Tato Fashion Club** (ⓐ Sofiyi Perovskoyi 6–11 ⓣ 456 1782 ⓦ www.tatoclub.com.ua ⓛ 20.00–06.00 ⓝ Metro: Shuliavska), which see models traipsing down a catwalk and then dancing with the patrons. **Azhur** (ⓐ Leontovycha 3 ⓣ 234 7494 ⓦ www.avalon.ua ⓛ 22.00–06.00 ⓝ Metro: Universytet) is the place to go if you want to shake your booty to the disco and pop classics of the 60s, 70s and 80s.

Although many of the city's nightclubs rely on industrial-sized speakers to pump out their tunes, others, such as Art Club 44, offer live music. Themed pubs and clubs are also to be found: there are a few Irish pubs in the centre as well as a German-style beer hall (see page 88).

If you fancy going a bit more highbrow, theatre, opera, ballet, concerts, puppet shows and, yes, the circus are excellent ways to pass an evening in Kiev. You may not understand the dialogue but there can be something magical about watching a play by Chekhov being performed in the country in which it was written. Part of the fun also comes from watching the other patrons, such as the families with young children, who come dressed up for the performance. Keep in mind that Kiev is a style-conscious city and it just won't do to dress down for a night on the town, no matter what the venue.

If the word 'ballet' conjures up the phrase 'not my thing', think again. Governments may rise and fall, but the ballet in Kiev hasn't

Festive celebrations at the Mariinsky Palace

WHERE TO BUY TICKETS

Central Box Office ⓐ Khreschatyk 21 ⓣ 234 6066 ⓦ www.ctk.kiev.ua ⓔ ctk.kiev@gmail.com Ⓜ Metro: Khreschatyk

You can also try the English-language online booking service at ⓦ www.parter.ua

Its not in English, but Karabas's adverts can also give you and idea of what is coming up ⓣ 590 5555 ⓦ www.karabas.com

faltered a single step in maintaining its high quality. Seeing a performance at this level of professionalism may well make you a ballet convert. Kiev's opera scene is equally fascinating and there are opportunities to see one almost every single night, as well as frequent matinées. To make it a truly local experience, try some caviar and toast at the intermission, and don't forget flowers for the ballerinas. (It's also okay to shout 'bravo' with gusto.) Classical music was once a fairly cheap outing in the city, but prices have been on the increase and availability on the decrease. Performances of either classical or folk music occur almost every night.

Looking for something completely different? Try the **National Circus of Ukraine** (ⓐ Peremohy pl. 3) or the **Kiev Academic Puppet Theatre** (ⓐ Hrushevskoho 1A). There's no need to worry about language difficulties with the circus – the glitz, the acrobatic feats and the animal acts speak their own language. Puppet performances are not just for children and there are several theatres that specialise in this type of entertainment. Puppets vary from the traditional marionettes to giant-sized creations.

Kiev's Taras Shevchenko National Opera & Ballet Theatre

Sport & relaxation

SPECTATOR SPORTS

The leading spectator sport in Kiev is football, and Dynamo Kiev is a famous and very successful club. Ukrainian football player Andriy Shevchenko is a national hero who was named European Footballer of the Year in 2004, and returned to Dynamo Kiev after stints at AC Milan and Chelsea. Dynamo Stadium, very close to the city centre, is the home of the team and is where all of its home matches are played. Tickets cost anything from 10hr. upwards and can be purchased at the stadium entrance. **Dynamo Stadium** Hrushevskoho 3 279 5272 www.fcdynamo.kiev.ua Metro: Maidan Nezalezhnosti

Olympic (Respublikansky) Stadium (Chervonoarmiyska (Velyka Vasylkivska) 55 246 7007 Metro: Respublikansky Stadion) is where Dynamo Kiev's European matches used to be played. It was fully reconstructed in 1980 as one of the Olympic

Hidropark is Kiev's main centre for outdoor activities

sites and is now undergoing another full-scale refurbishment as a major venue for Euro 2012 matches. When re-opened, it will hold around 70,000 people, as opposed to Dynamo Stadium's 15,000. Delays in the renovation had panicked UEFA, prompting suggestions that some or all of Ukraine's matches could be switched elsewhere. However, it now looks like work will be finished on time, and the Ukrainians are eagerly awaiting the competition, to be co-hosted with Poland.

Boxing has become another popular spectator sport, especially since two Ukrainian brothers, Vitali ('Doctor Ironfist') and Wladimir Klitschko have achieved international prominence.

Winter sports such as ice hockey, skiing and ice-skating are very popular. Ukraine has produced a number of Olympic champions, especially in hockey and figure skating.

PARTICIPATION SPORTS

Summer activities centre around the River Dnipro. Boating is a favourite, as Kyivans take to the waters of the Dnipro to cool down from the summer heat. Boat rides of one to two hours are available at the boat terminal at Poshtova ploscha in Podil.

Hidropark, accessed by the metro station of the same name, is a recreation area built on two islands in the middle of the river. It features sandy beaches, and trails through forests and marshes. Swimming in the river is not recommended because of pollution; however there are two swimming pools on site. Amusement rides, a volleyball court, a nightclub and food vendors can also be found there.

Ice fishing is a curious winter activity. Fishermen chop a hole in the ice on the river, and drop in a baited line. They also normally consume large quantities of vodka, used as anti-freeze against the cold winds blowing on the river.

Accommodation

The price and quality of Kiev's many hotels run the gamut from outstanding to vile. The standard three- or four-star rating system does not work well in Kiev, as hotels with wonderful lobbies and restaurants can have miserable rooms upstairs. Pricing is not always a good indicator of quality either, as it seems to depend on what proprietors think they can get. Timid travellers may want to stick to the hotels of well-established international chains. In any case, be sure to see your room and have a settled price before checking in.

HOTELS

Central Railway Station £ Kiev's main station has overnight rooms in both of its terminals available for those arriving late or departing early. The rooms are pleasant enough and there is Internet access, but bathrooms are shared. You cannot reserve these rooms but may inquire about their immediate availability by phone. ⓐ Vokzalna pl. 2 (Central Kiev) ⓣ 465 2111

Holosiyvsky £–££ Located in the south of the city. Rooms are cheap, but you get what you pay for. ⓐ Holosiyvsky prosp. 93 (Outer Kiev)

PRICE CATEGORIES

Price categories represent the average price for two people sharing a double room for one night. Breakfast is often included.
£ up to 400 hr. **££** 400–700 hr. **£££** 700–1200 hr.
££££ over 1200 hr.

259 7672 www.hotelgolos.kiev.ua Metro: Holosiivska, then trolley bus: 2, 4, 11, 12, 14

Druzhba ££ In the southern part of town, close to the Lybidska metro station. Druzhby Narodiv bul. 5 (Outer Kiev) 528 3300 www.hotel-druzhba.com.ua Metro: Lybidska

Express ££ This hotel is near the main railway station, and contains the central booking office for the railway system. The interior is quite nice, although the exterior is rather stark. Tarasa Shevchenka bul. 38–40 (Central Kiev) 503 3045 www.expresskiev.com Metro: Universytet

Myr ££ In the south of the city, very near the central bus station, this is a Soviet-style high-rise. The hotel is well kept but the rooms can be small. Holosiivskyi prosp. 70 (Outer Kiev) 520 26019 www.hotelmir.kiev.ua Metro: Holosiivska

Tourist ££ Kiev's largest hotel complex looks like a Russian apartment block on the outside. It is nicer inside. Located on the left bank, it is close to the Livoberezhna metro station, the river and Hidropark. It features restaurants, Internet access, a bar and a tourist office. If you do not mind riding the metro into town, the rooms are good value. Rayisy Okipnoyi 2 (Outer Kiev) 568 4254 www.hotel-tourist.kiev.ua Metro: Livoberezhna

Adria £££ This is part of the Tourist Hotel complex, but far more luxurious. The complex boasts restaurants, Internet access, a bar and a tourist office. Rayisy Okipnoyi 2 (Outer Kiev) 568 4457 www.adria.kiev.ua Metro: Livoberezhna

APARTMENTS

Although it's not the first solution that a tourist might think of, renting an apartment – even for a very short stay – can be a more economical and comfortable option than a mid-range hotel, decent examples of which are not abundant in Kiev. Various agents – usually English speaking – can help you find somewhere. Don't forget to check the location, availability of hot water and central heating, and whom to contact in a property-related emergency. ⓦ www.bestkievapartment.com, www.teren.kiev.ua, www.ukr-apartments.kiev.ua

Boatel Dniprovsky £££ A unique hotel floating on the River Dnipro in the Podil area of the city. ⓐ Naberezhno-Khreschatytska 10A, moorage 2 (Podil) ⓣ 490 9055 ⓦ www.dneprovskiy.kiev.ua Ⓜ Metro: Poshtova Ploscha

Domus £££ In the centre of Podil, this smart-looking hotel features an Italian restaurant. ⓐ Yaroslavska 19 (Podil) ⓣ 490 9009 ⓦ www.domus-hotel.kiev.ua Ⓜ Metro: Kontraktova Ploscha

Hotel Gintama £££ A small, friendly hotel, this place is near St Alexander's Catholic Church in the centre of the city. ⓐ Triokhsviatytelska 9 (Central Kiev) ⓣ 278 5092 ⓦ www.gintama.com.ua Ⓜ Metro: Maidan Nezalezhnosti

Khreschatyk £££ Located in the centre of town, the Khreschatyk has comfortable rooms but can be noisy. ⓐ Khreschatyk 14 (Central Kiev) ⓣ 596 8004 ⓦ www.khreschatik.kiev.ua Ⓜ Metro: Maidan Nezalezhnosti

Kiev £££ Close to the Ukrainian Parliament, the Kiev normally serves as its members' dwelling house. It features a bar, restaurant, banquet halls and shops, and there's a good park just over the road. ⓐ Hrushevskoho 26/1 (Pechersk) ⓣ 253 0155 ⓦ www.hotelkiev.com.ua Ⓝ Metro: Arsenalna

Kozatskiy £££ Located in the centre of the city, overlooking the Maidan Nezalezhnosti. ⓐ Mykhailivska 1–3 (Central Kiev) ⓣ 279 4925 ⓦ www.kozatskiy.kiev.ua Ⓝ Metro: Maidan Nezalezhnosti

Lybid £££ Conveniently located next to the railway station and Ukraina shopping mall, this hotel has everything you could want, including a business centre, bar and casino. ⓐ Peremohy pl. 1 (Central Kiev) ⓣ 236 0063 ⓦ www.hotellybid.com.ua Ⓝ Metro: Vokzalna

Rus £££ Rus is a leading hotel in Kiev and is lavishly decorated with mosaics and sculptures. It contains a convention centre, a restaurant, three bars (including a sushi bar) and two banqueting halls, but the rooms are reasonably priced. It is located near the Olympic stadium in the city centre. ⓐ Hospitalna 4 (Central Kiev) ⓣ 256 4000 ⓦ www.hotelrus.kiev.ua Ⓝ Metro: Palats Sportu

Salute £££ This distinctive cylindrical hotel is just north of the Caves Monastery. ⓐ Ivana Mazepy (Sichnevoho Povstannia) 11A (Pechersk) ⓣ 449 1420 ⓦ www.salutehotel.kiev.ua Ⓝ Metro: Arsenalna

Vozdvyzhensky £££ This small hotel is near the city centre, but its location away from the busy streets ensures that its rooms are quiet. ⓐ Vozdvyzhenska 60A/B (Podil) ⓣ 531 9900 ⓦ www.vozdvyzhensky.com Ⓝ Metro: Kontraktova Ploscha

Dnipro ££££ This luxury hotel is a leftover from the Soviet era; in fact only the suites and larger rooms are luxurious, the standard rooms being rather small. It does, however, have an outstanding restaurant. ⓐ Khreschatyk 1/2 (Central Kiev) ⓣ 254 6777 ⓦ www.dniprohotel.ua ⓜ Metro: Maidan Nezalezhnosti

Hyatt Regency Kiev ££££ One of the newest five-star hotels in Kiev, this place has 234 rooms, including 25 suites overlooking one of the main Kiev attractions, St Sophia's Cathedral. The hotel has a fitness centre with swimming pool, a business centre and a car-hire office.

The impressive Hyatt Regency Kiev is situated in a prime location in the city

ⓐ Tarasovoyi 5, off Sofiyska Square (Central Kiev) ⓣ 581 1234 ⓦ http://kiev.regency.hyatt.com ⓜ Metro: Maidan Nezalezhnosti

Impressa ££££ Luxurious and very clean, this small hotel in the centre of the Podil area features an on-site casino. ⓐ Sahaydachnoho 21 (Podil) ⓣ 239 2939 ⓦ www.impressa.com.ua ⓜ Metro: Poshtova Ploscha

Natsionalny ££££ Popular hotel near Parliament. ⓐ Lypska 5 (Pechersk) ⓣ 255 8888 ⓦ www.natsionalny.kiev.ua ⓜ Metro: Khreschatyk or Arsenalna

Premier Palace ££££ Some consider this to be Kiev's most impressive hotel. Located in the centre of the city, it offers a health club, a business centre and excellent service. ⓐ Tarasa Shevchenka bul. 5–7 (Central Kiev) ⓣ 244 1200, 537 4500 ⓦ www.premier-palace.com ⓜ Metro: Ploscha Lva Tolstoho

Radisson Blu ££££ Known for its high standards of service, the Radisson Blu is located to the west of the city centre. ⓐ Yaroslaviv Val 22 (Central Kiev) ⓣ 492 2200 ⓦ www.radissonblu.com/hotel-kiev ⓜ Metro: Zoloti Vorota

HOSTELS

Kiev International Youth Hostel £ This hostel has a 24-hour reception with English-speaking staff and is close to a metro station. ⓐ Artema 52A (Central Kiev) ⓣ 481 3838 ⓦ www.hostelworld.com ⓜ Metro: Lukyanivska

Yaroslav International Youth Hostel £ Located in the historic Podil area, this hostel has English-speaking staff. ⓐ Yaroslavska 10 (Podil) ⓣ 331 0260 ⓦ www.hostelworld.com ⓜ Metro: Kontraktova Ploscha

THE BEST OF KIEV

TOP 10 ATTRACTIONS

- **Kievo-Pecherska Lavra (The Caves Monastery)** The most popular attraction in Kiev. If you see nothing else, you must visit this (see page 90).

- **Khreschatyk & Maidan Nezalezhnosti (Independence Square)** The source of some of the city's most exciting events (see pages 73 & 74).

- **Andriivsky uzviz (Andrew's Descent)** There's a lot to see and do on this street, whether it's visiting St Andrew's Church or buying all your souvenirs here (see page 70).

- **Podil** This small (but perfectly formed) corner of Kiev offers a host of great things to see, do and devour (see page 100).

- **Cathedrals** Sofiysky Sobor (St Sophia's) is Kiev's most beautiful church. St Volodymyr's is where you should go to join the Kyivans for an Orthodox service – a truly moving experience (see page 76).

An easter-egg sculpture at the Caves Monastery

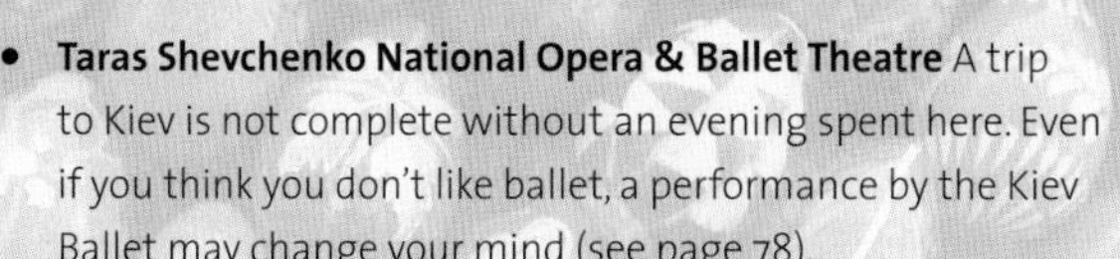

- **Taras Shevchenko National Opera & Ballet Theatre** A trip to Kiev is not complete without an evening spent here. Even if you think you don't like ballet, a performance by the Kiev Ballet may change your mind (see page 78).

- **Babi Yar** No one can fail to be affected by this memorial to the victims of Nazi genocide (see page 109).

- **The Desiatynna Church Ruins & National History Museum** This ruined church was destroyed by a Mongol invasion in 1240; the fascinating museum nearby is the best place to get a feel for the country's rich and colourful history (see pages 70 & 78).

- **Pyrohovo Open-air Museum of Folk Architecture & Life** A good place to learn about the daily life of people who lived in the Ukrainian countryside in times past. The museum is actually made up of 300 separate buildings arranged in the form of a traditional village (see page 114).

- **Chornobyl (Chernobyl)** The site of the nuclear disaster is no chuckle-fest, but it's still a must-see destination (see page 110).

Suggested itineraries

HALF-DAY: KIEV IN A HURRY

In the morning, try to get to the Caves Monastery (see page 90). Go as early as possible, and go to the Lower Lavra. If you have time after visiting the caves, then start to explore the Upper Lavra.

If caves are not your thing and you want to see some of the city, then the following walk will take you round many of the best central sights. Start by walking round Maidan Nezalezhnosti (Independence Square, see page 74), with its statues, monuments and fountains, and then head south down the east side of Khreschatyk. Look out for the big TsUM store across the street at the intersection of Bohdana Khmelnytskoho. Where Khreschatyk intersects with Tarasa Shevchenka bulvar, you will find the Besarabsky market. Cross under the street to Tarasa Shevchenka and continue west.

A short side trip south on Volodymyrska will take you to Kiev University. At the intersection of Ivana Franka, you will find the **Fomin Botanic Gardens** (ⓐ Kominterna 1 ⓜ Metro: Universytet) on your left and St Volodymyr's Cathedral (see page 76) on your right. From here it's a short walk to the Taras Shevchenko National Opera and Ballet Theatre (see page 78). Continue north on Volodymyrska, and you will pass the Golden Gate and St Sophia's Cathedral (see page 76). At Sophia's Square, stay on Volodymyrska until you reach Desiatynna, where you will find the Desiatynna ruins and St Andrew's Church.

After a frenetic couple of hours, find an outdoor café, sit down and have a nice cold Ukrainian beer and a bowl of *borsch*!

1 DAY: TIME TO SEE A LITTLE MORE

Start early in the morning to avoid the crowds, and head for the Caves Monastery. Start with the Lower Lavra and the caves themselves, then

explore the Upper Lavra. Return to Maidan Nezalezhnosti for a light lunch, and then take the half-day walking tour already suggested. Depending on time and stamina, you may take a side trip down Andrew's Descent (see page 70) into Kontraktova ploscha in Podil. Explore the square, then continue east on Sahaydachnoho and take the funicular up to St Michael's Golden-Domed Monastery (see page 75).

Finish the day with a leisurely meal at one of the riverfront restaurants in Podil.

2–3 DAYS: TIME TO SEE MUCH MORE

After you have done the one-day activities, take some time to go back to explore the museums and churches that interest you, walk around Podil, shop for souvenirs on Andrew's Descent, and attend a performance of the opera or ballet. Other experiences would be a trip to Babi Yar (see page 109), attending an Orthodox church service, strolling through either of the Botanic Gardens, or joining the shopping crowd in Besarabsky market or Kontraktova ploscha. Pick up some bread, cheese and wine at one of the many supermarkets, and go to Hidropark to enjoy a picnic lunch on the banks of the river. In the evening, choose between a memorable night at the opera or ballet and a (probably less memorable) few hours at one of Kiev's nightclubs.

LONGER: ENJOYING KIEV TO THE FULL

If you have longer, and you have seen all you want to see in Kiev, then plan a day trip to Chernobyl (see page 110), or to the Pyrohovo Open-air Museum of Folk Architecture & Life (see page 114). For a complete contrast, take an overnight train ride to Lviv (see page 116), another beautiful but quite different Ukrainian city, well worth visiting for a few days.

Something for nothing

One advantage of visiting Kiev is that many of the sights and attractions are free, or have a very small admission fee.

Kiev is a city of churches, many of which have recently been renovated, and, as they are still owned by the church, are open to the public. There is usually no entrance fee to churches, although visitors are expected to purchase a candle, which costs from 1–3hr. Other churches have been converted to museums and, although there is an entrance fee, it is usually quite low – 10hr. or less.

The main attraction in Kiev is the Caves Monastery. Although there is an entrance fee to the monastery complex, entrance to the caves themselves is free. You can avoid paying the fee by going directly to the Lower Lavra entrance, just south of the main entrance.

Central Kiev and Podil are fairly compact, making them quite walkable. It costs nothing to walk the streets to view the buildings, monuments and statues, and to enjoy the many parks. It is possible to get a feel for the city and its culture without having to pay anything.

Free attractions in Kiev that are definitely worth a visit include the huge PinchukArtCentre (see page 78), Mykhailivsky Zolotoverkhy Monastery (see page 75), St Volodymyr's Cathedral (see page 76) and the sobering Babi Yar (see page 109), which commemorates Ukrainian citizens murdered by the Nazis in World War II. St Andrew's Church and the Desiatynna Church Ruins (see page 70) are both free to visit, as are Vydubytsky Monastery (see page 97) and Pokrovska Convent (see page 112).

Other worthwhile attractions have only a small admission charge of 10hr. or less. Among these are the National Museum of Chernobyl (see page 103), the Museum of One Street (see page 104) and the Museum of the Great Patriotic War (see page 97). The grounds of St Sophia's Cathedral are also free to walk around (see page 76).

Stroll among ancient churches and monasteries

When it rains

There's no need to despair for lack of things to do in Kiev when the weather turns dismal. You'll discover a wealth of activities and experiences inside many of the city's great treasures.

If it rains (or snows) on a Sunday, or any other day, go to church. St Volodymyr's Cathedral (see page 76) is one of the most artistic churches in the city. Built in the Byzantine style, it has a bright yellow exterior capped by seven blue domes dotted with golden stars. Inside, the walls are covered with paintings depicting the spiritual history of the city. You can combine the beauty of an Orthodox service with your sightseeing. St Volodymyr's is a favourite church for Kyivans, making this a truly authentic experience. Services are held on weekdays at 08.00 and 17.00, and at 07.00, 10.00 and 17.00 at the weekend. The church is open to the public from 06.00–19.30.

Inclement days are perfect for the interiors of museums. The National History Museum (see page 78) provides an excellent overview of Ukrainian history from prehistoric times to the present. The collections are wide and varied, including books, art, artefacts, archaeological finds and even coins.

If it must be art and art alone for your dreary day, head to the National Art Museum (see page 78). The collection inside is largely unknown to the Western world and you'll be in for a few surprises. Most of the works are by Ukrainian artists and span a time period from the 14th to the 20th centuries.

Meteorological conditions can even force you underground! Or is that just another excuse to go shopping? Globus is a lively underground shopping centre, featuring lots of recognisable Western labels such as Polo and Esprit. The stores are open from 10.00 to 22.00 so you can spend as long as you or your wallet hold out.

Metrograd is another underground shopping centre worthy of exploration: in general the prices and quality are lower than those at Globus. For a truly posh experience, head for Mandarin Plaza – this is where the Kyivan upper crust comes to shop for designer fashions from around the world.

And, of course, there are always movies, plays, puppet shows, concerts and operas to keep you both amused and dry.

Swap your umbrella for the shelter of the Globus shopping centre

On arrival

TIME DIFFERENCE

Ukraine is on Eastern European Time (EET), two hours ahead of GMT in winter. Daylight Saving applies: clocks go forward one hour on the last Sunday in March and fall back one hour on the last Sunday in October.

ARRIVING

By air

Most international flights arrive at **Kiev Boryspil State International Airport** (585 7254 www.kbp.com.ua), which is 35 km (22 miles) east of the city. Expect to spend up to an hour clearing customs and immigration (for visa requirements, see page 141). The airport is small but modern and has bureaux de change, ATMs, duty-free shopping, a post office and telephones. There is also a bar that has Internet access and a Wi-Fi hotspot. You should obtain some local currency on arrival, as taxis and shops may not take euros, dollars or credit cards (see page 144).

To get into Kiev you can catch the Polit/Atass bus in front of the international arrivals terminal. The trip to Kiev's central railway station takes up to an hour and costs 30hr. Alternatively, get off the bus at Kharkivska metro station at the entrance to the city and take the metro into town – this will cost only about 20hr. and almost certainly be quicker. Buses leave every 15–30 minutes, 05.00–01.00. You can also take a taxi, which costs 200–300hr. and takes 30–45 minutes. An express rail link was planned for Euro 2012, but is likely to miss its deadline.

Kiev Zhuliany Airport (www.airport.kiev.ua), located closer to the city centre, is being upgraded ready for Euro 2012 and is now the local base for low-cost operator Wizz Air. It also handles domestic flights.

By rail

Kiev's refurbished and extended Central Railway Station is fairly smart and user-friendly, with bilingual signage in English and Cyrillic. There are bureaux de change, ATMs and public phones. The station has overnight rooms to rent (see page 44) for those arriving late or departing early. The rooms are inexpensive, clean and secure, and there is Wi-Fi access, although the bathrooms are shared.

The station is close to the centre of town. Although you can walk, you may want to take a taxi, metro, trolleybus, bus or minibus. Taxis

Kiev is rightly proud of its modernised railway station

tend to overcharge people picked up at the railway station but you can avoid this by calling a taxi by phone (see page 68).

Central Railway Station ⓐ Vokzalna pl. 1 ⓣ 503 7005

By road

All international and national buses stop at the central bus station, although many incoming buses will stop at other bus terminals that may be closer to your destination in Kiev. The central bus station is badly in need of renovation, so do not plan to spend any time there. There is a bureau de change, an ATM, a café and public phones. The central bus station is in the southern part of the city. You can take a taxi or a trolleybus (lines 2, 4, 11 or 12) into the city centre and the Lybidska metro station is nearby.

Driving to Kiev is only for the brave. Highway E-40 runs from Western Europe directly into Kiev. Driving in the city can be difficult, as street signs are in Cyrillic and are posted on buildings in positions that are often hard to see. Although the streets are in generally good condition, there is no logic to their layout and they are often closed for celebrations. You will also find some rather rough tram-track crossings. Construction zones are poorly marked and can prove dangerous, especially at night. Parking is also a problem in Kiev. There are state-owned car parks around the city; you should only park in designated spots, and in areas that are well lit and secure.

Central Bus Station ⓐ Moskovska pl. 3 ⓣ 527 9986 Ⓜ Metro: Lybidska

FINDING YOUR FEET

Few people in Kiev speak English and most signs are in Cyrillic, so you will want to stay in the city centre and Podil, which are the major tourist areas and where most English is spoken. As you get further from the city centre, the underlying poverty becomes more

IF YOU GET LOST, TRY . . .

Excuse me. Do you speak English?
Перепрошую. Ви розмовляєте англійською?
Pereproshuyu. Vy rozmovlyayete anhliys'koyu?

Excuse me, is this the right way to . . . ?
Вибачте, я правильно йду до . . . ?
Vybachte, ya pravyl'no ydu do . . . ?

Can you point to it on my map?
Ви можете показати де це на карті?
Vy mozhete pokazaty de tse na karti?

obvious, fewer and fewer people speak English, and facilities that can help or cater for visitors become rarer.

ORIENTATION

Maidan Nezalezhnosti, or Independence Square, is the centre of the city, and the meeting place in Kiev. It is a good place to start any exploration of the city. Maidan Nezalezhnosti lies on Khreschatyk, a wide street that runs southwest past the square towards the Olympic Stadium. To the east and southeast of Maidan Nezalezhnosti are the parks that line the River Dnipro, and then the river itself, Hidropark and the left bank.

About 1 km (⅔ mile) north of Maidan Nezalezhnosti are the funicular and stairways that take you down into Podil and to the banks of the River Dnipro. South of Maidan Nezalezhnosti is the

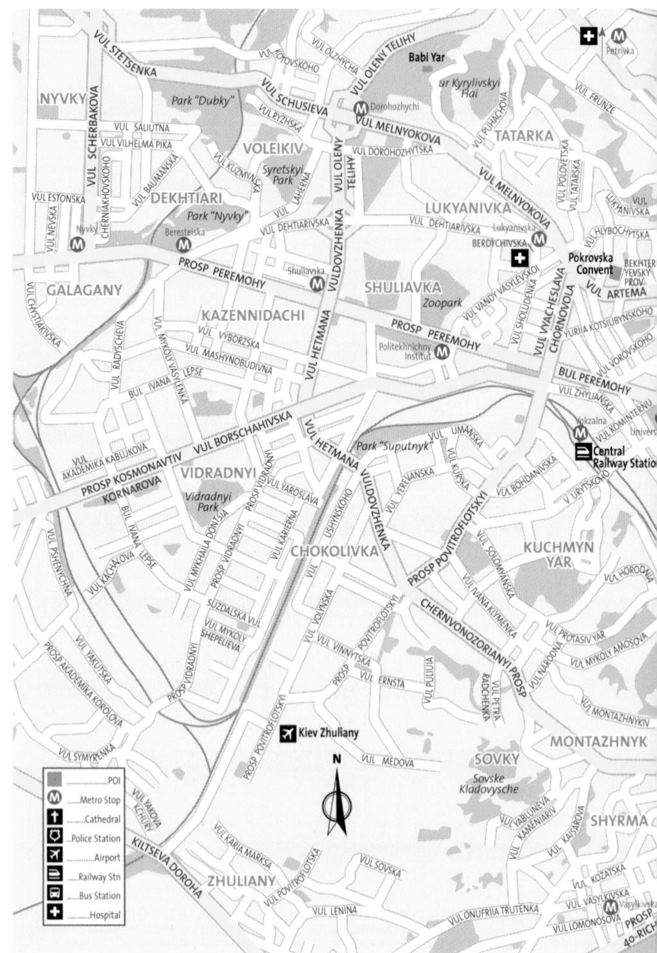
VUL STETSENKA
VUL KOTOVSKOHO
VUL OLZHYCHA
VUL OLENY TELIHY
Babi Yar
ur Kyrylivskyi Hai
Petrivka
VUL FRUNZE
NYVKY
Park "Dubky"
VUL SCHUSIEVA
VUL RYZHSKA
Dorohozhychi
VUL MELNYOKOVA
VUL PUHACHOVA
TATARKA
VUL SCHERBAKOVA
VUL SALIUTNA
VUL VILHELMA PIKA
VOLEIKIV
VUL DOROHOZHYTSKA
VUL KUZMYNSKA
Syretskyi Park
VUL OLENY TELIHY
VUL LAHERNA
VUL POLOVETSKA
VUL TATARSKA
VUL BAUMANSKA
CHERNIAKHOVSKOHO
VUL ESTONSKA
DEKHTIARI
Park "Nyvky"
LUKYANIVKA
VUL DEHTIARIVSKA
VUL NEVSKA
Nyvky
Beresteiska
Lukyanivska
BERDYCHIVSKA
VUL LUKYANIVSKA
VUL HLYBOCHYTSKA
Pokrovska Convent
BEKHTEREVSKY PROV
VUL ARTEMA
PROSP PEREMOHY
Shuliavska
VUL DOVZHENKA
SHULIAVKA
Zoopark
VUL VANDY VASYLEVSKOI
VUL SHOLUDENKA
VUL VYACHESLAVA CHORNOVOLA
YURIIA KOTSIUBYNSKOHO
VUL VOROVSKOHO
GALAGANY
VUL CHYSTIAKIVSKA
KAZENNIDACHI
VUL VYBORZSKA
VUL MASHYNOBUDIVNA
VUL RADYSCHEVA
VUL MYKOLY VASYLENKA
BUL IVANA LEPSE
VUL HETMANA
Politekhnichny Instytut
BUL PEREMOHY
VUL ZHYLIANSKA
Vokzalna
VUL KOMINTERNU
Univers
Central Railway Statio
VUL BORSCHAHIVSKA
VUL HETMANA
Park "Suputnyk"
VUL UMANSKA
VUL AKADEMIKA KABLUKOVA
PROSP KOSMONAVTIV KOMAROVA
VIDRADNYI
PROSP VIDRADNYI
VUL YAROSLAVA
VUL YEREVANSKA
VUL KURSKA
VUL BOHDANIVSKA
V URYTSKOHO
Vidradnyi Park
VUL DOVZHENKA
PROSP POVITROFLOTSKYI
BUL IVANA LEPSE
VUL MYKHAILA DONTSIA
VUL KARIERNA
VUL USHYNSKOHO
VUL SOLOMYANSKA
KUCHMYN YAR
VUL PSHENYCHNA
VUL KACHALOVA
CHOKOLIVKA
VUL HORODNIA
SUZDALSKA VUL
VUL MYKOLY SHEPELIEVA
VUL VOLYNSKA
VUL IVANA KLYMENKA
CHERNVONOZORIANYI PROSP
VUL PROTASIV YAR
VUL MYKOLY AMOSOVA
VUL VINNYTSKA
VUL ERNSTA
VUL PULIUIA
VUL PETRA RADCHENKA
VUL NARODNA
VUL YAKUTSKA
PROSP AKADEMIKA KOROLOVA
VUL MONTAZHNYKIV
MONTAZHNYK
Kiev Zhuliany
N
VUL MEDOVA
SOVKY
Sovske Kladovysche
VUL SYMYRENKA
VUL YAKOVA KCHURY
VUL YABLUNEVA
VUL KAMENIARIV
VUL KAISAROVA
SHYRMA
KILTSEVA DOROHA
VUL KARLA MARKSA
VUL SOVSKA
VUL KOZATSKA
ZHULIANY
VUL POVITROFLOTSKA
VUL LENINA
VUL ONUFRIIA TRUTENKA
VUL VASYLKIVSKA
Vasylkivska
VUL LOMONOSOVA
PROSP 40-RICH
POI
Metro Stop
Cathedral
Police Station
Airport
Railway Stn
Bus Station
Hospital

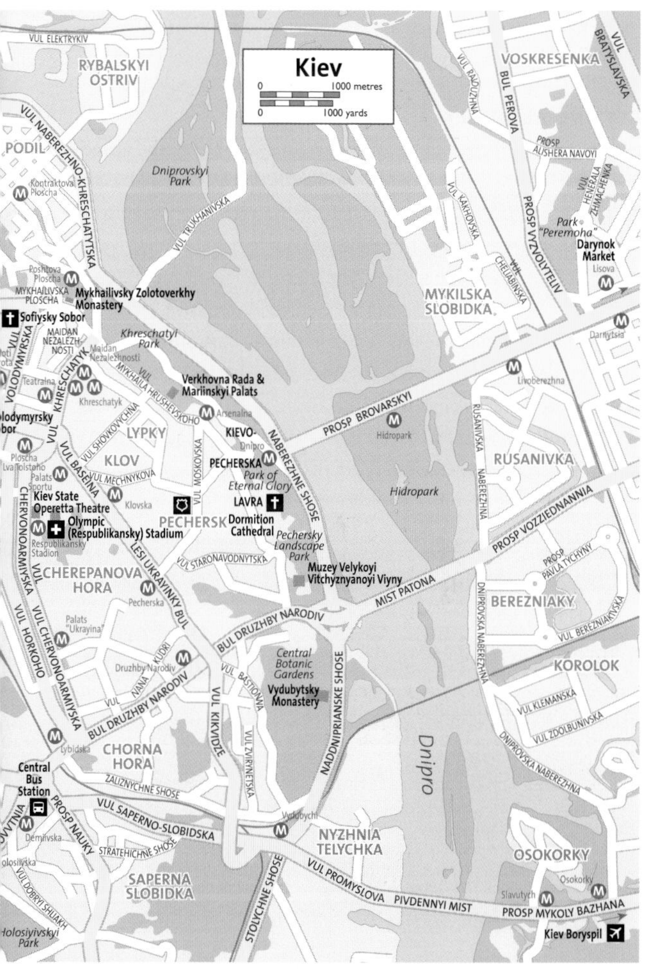
Kiev
0
1000 metres
0
1000 yards
VUL ELEKTRYKIV
RYBALSKYI OSTRIV
PODIL
VUL NABEREZHNO-KHRESCHATYTSKA
Kontraktova Ploscha
Dniprovskyi Park
VUL TRUKHANIVSKA
Poshtova Ploscha
MYKHAILIVSKA PLOSCHA
Mykhailivsky Zolotoverkhy Monastery
Sofiysky Sobor
MAIDAN NEZALEZH-NOSTI
Maidan Nezalezhnosti
Khreschatyi Park
VUL VOLODYMYRSKA
Teatralna
VUL KHRESCHATYK
Khreschatyk
VUL MYKHAILA HRUSHEVSKOHO
Verkhovna Rada & Mariinskyi Palats
Arsenalna
VUL SHOVKOVYCHNA
LYPKY
KLOV
VUL MOSKOVSKA
KIEVO-PECHERSKA
Dnipro
Ploscha Lva Tolstoho
Palats Sportu
VUL BASEINA
VUL MECHNYKOVA
Kiev State Operetta Theatre
Klovska
Park of Eternal Glory
LAVRA
NABEREZHNE SHOSE
Olympic (Respublikansky) Stadium
Respublikansky Stadion
PECHERSK
Dormition Cathedral
Pechersky Landscape Park
VUL CHERVONOARMIYSKA
CHEREPANOVA HORA
VUL STARONAVODNYTSKA
LESI UKRAYINKY BUL
Muzey Velykoyi Vitchyznyanoyi Viyny
Pecherska
Palats "Ukrayina"
VUL HORKOHO
VUL CHERVONOARMIYSKA
BUL DRUZHBY NARODIV
Druzhby Narodiv
VUL NANA KUDRI
VUL BASTIONNA
Central Botanic Gardens
Vydubytsky Monastery
NADDNIPRIANSKE SHOSE
VUL KIKVIDZE
VUL ZVIRYNETSKA
Lybidska
CHORNA HORA
Central Bus Station
ZALIZNYCHNE SHOSE
VUL SAPERNO-SLOBIDSKA
PROSP NAUKY
Demiivska
STRATEHICHNE SHOSE
Vydubychi
NYZHNIA TELYCHKA
VUL DOBRYI SHLIAKH
SAPERNA SLOBIDKA
STOLYCHNE SHOSE
VUL PROMYSLOVA
PIVDENNYI MIST
Holosiyivskyi Park
VUL RAIDUZHNA
BUL PEROVA
VOSKRESENKA
VUL BRATYSLAVSKA
PROSP ALISHERA NAVOYI
VUL HENERALA ZHMACHENKA
VUL KAKHOVSKA
PROSP VYZVOLYTELIV
Park "Peremoha"
Darynok Market
Lisova
VUL CHELIABINSKA
MYKILSKA SLOBIDKA
Darnytsia
Livoberezhna
PROSP BROVARSKYI
Hidropark
RUSANIVSKA
RUSANIVKA
NABEREZHNA
Hidropark
PROSP VOZZIEDNANNIA
PROSP PAVLA TYCHYNY
MIST PATONA
DNIPROVSKA NABEREZHNA
BEREZNIAKY
VUL BEREZNIAKIVSKA
KOROLOK
VUL KLEMANSKA
VUL ZDOLBUNIVSKA
Dnipro
DNIPROVSKA NABEREZHNA
OSOKORKY
Osokorky
Slavutych
PROSP MYKOLY BAZHANA
Kiev Boryspil

historic area of Pechersk, with the Parliament buildings and the Caves Monastery.

GETTING AROUND

Kiev is a very large city, but fortunately most of the sights and attractions are within 2 km (1¼ miles) of Maidan Nezalezhnosti, and many within half that distance, so walking is feasible for most sightseeing.

If you want to wander further than your feet can take you, Kiev has a good public transport system. The metro (subway) has three lines, and is fast, clean and reliable, not to mention inexpensive.

But, partly due to the low cost, the central part of the metro is overcrowded throughout the day, and the other sections are overcrowded during rush hours. Be aware of numerous pickpockets who pretend to help you to get inside a carriage while stealing your belongings. One ride costs only 2hr., but you need to purchase blue tokens available from the station entrances. Signs are in Cyrillic, so

be sure you know where you are going before you start. Look on carriage windows for metro maps in both Ukrainian and English.

Although most of the metro system is underground, the first (red) line on the left bank of the Dnipro lies on the surface, and you can observe the river and the central part of Kiev while crossing the bridge between Dnipro and Livoberezhna stations.

Buses, trolleybuses and trams can also get you around, but heavy traffic makes them better only for short hops. Tickets are 1.50hr. and can be purchased from drivers, conductors or street kiosks.

Marshrutkas are a cross between a bus and a taxi. They are minibuses, usually Mercedes or yellow Bohdan vans that use regular bus stops. They are much quicker than buses and trams, but cost more – anything from 2hr. upwards. They can also be very crowded so you may be forced to ride standing up.

Ornate arches tower overhead in Zoloti Vorota metro station

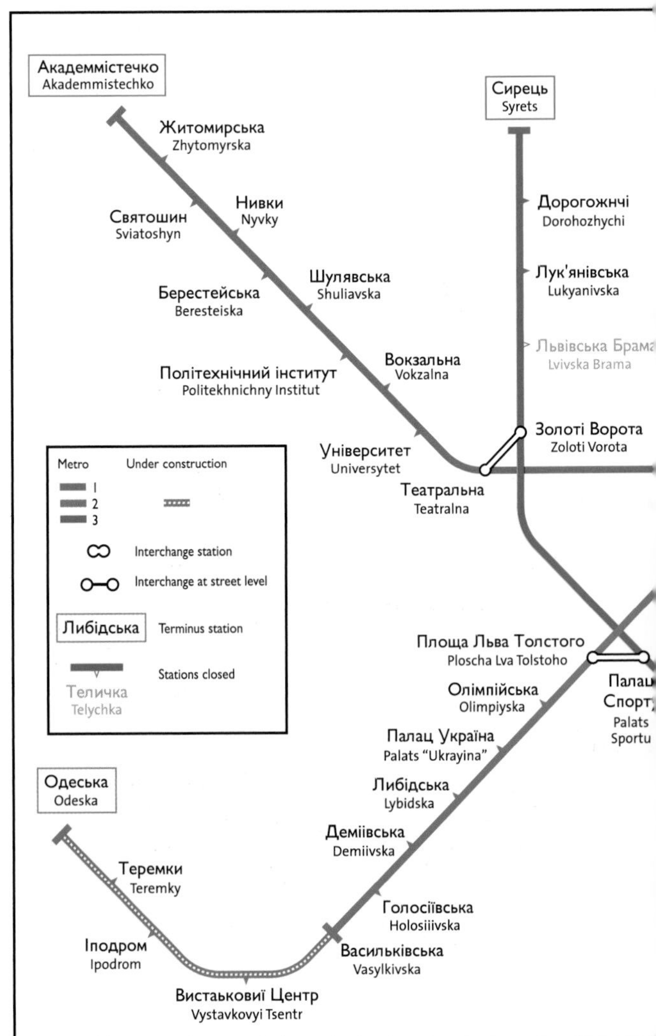
Академмістечко
Akademmistechko
Житомирська
Zhytomyrska
Святошин
Sviatoshyn
Нивки
Nyvky
Берестейська
Beresteiska
Шулявська
Shuliavska
Політехнічний інститут
Politekhnichny Institut
Вокзальна
Vokzalna
Університет
Universytet
Театральна
Teatralna
Сирець
Syrets
Дорогожичі
Dorohozhychi
Лук'янівська
Lukyanivska
Lvivska Brama
Золоті Ворота
Zoloti Vorota
Metro
Under construction
1
2
3
Interchange station
Interchange at street level
Либідська
Terminus station
Stations closed
Теличка
Telychka
Площа Льва Толстого
Ploscha Lva Tolstoho
Олімпійська
Olimpiyska
Палац Україна
Palats "Ukrayina"
Либідська
Lybidska
Деміївська
Demiivska
Голосіївська
Holosiivska
Васильківська
Vasylkivska
Одеська
Odeska
Теремки
Teremky
Іподром
Ipodrom
Виставкові Центр
Vystavkovyi Tsentr
Palats
Sportu

A Communicarta Style45 design
© Communicarta Ltd 2007-2011 UDN.2a
Map user Ref: WZFG/CS/KBP/2011/1
Героїв Дніпра
Heroyiv Dnipra
Мінська
Minska
Оболонь
Obolon
Петрівка
Petrivka
Тараса Шевченка
Tarasa Shevchenka
Фунікулер
Funikuler
Контрактова Площа
Kontraktova Ploscha
Поштова Площа
Poshtova Ploscha
Майдан Незалежності
Maidan Nezalezhnosti
Хрещатик
Khreschatyk
Арсенальна
Arsenalna
Дніпро
Dnipro
Dnipro
Гідропарк
Hidropark
Лівобережна
Livoberezhna
Дарниця
Darnytsia
Чернігівська
Chernihivska
Лісова
Lisova
Червоний Хутір
Chervonyi
Бориспільська
Boryspilska
Харківська
Kharkivska
Вирлиця
Vyrlytsia
Осокорки
Osokorky
Позняки
Pozniaky
Славутич
Slavutych
Кловська
Klovska
Печерська
Pecherska
Дружби Народів
Druzhby Narodiv
Видубичі
Vydubychi
Теличка
Telychka

Taxis are ubiquitous in Kiev's streets, although few of the ones that you can hail are metered. Cabbies here drive like crazy and have flexible pricing policies, so settle on a price before you climb into the taxi, then hang on and pray. Usually a trip within the city centre costs around 50hr. If you do prefer a metered cab, go for **Taxi Partner** (ⓣ 234 4444/247 0000).

It is normally both safer and cheaper to phone for a taxi. One of the most reliable taxi companies is **Etalon Taxi** (ⓣ 501 5501/502 5454), but you can also call a cab from a landline by dialling 1554 or 1559. These companies should tell you the total cost before you make the trip.

Car hire

Daily rates are very high, as is insurance. It is wiser to stick with the big international rental agencies, and be sure to have lots of insurance as car thieves favour rental cars. Most car rental agencies offer chauffeur services, which may be worth the extra cost if you just want to sightsee by car.

Avis ⓐ Yamska 72 & Boryspil Airport ⓣ Town: 502 2010; airport: 591 7009 ⓦ www.avis.com.ua ⓛ 08.00–17.00 Mon–Fri

Europcar ⓐ Horkoho 48A & Boryspil Airport ⓣ Town: 238 2691; airport: 281 7737 ⓦ www.europcar.ua ⓛ 09.00–18.00 Mon–Fri

Hertz Rent A Car ⓐ Zdolbunivska 7D & Boryspil Airport ⓣ Town: 492 3270; airport: 281 7616 ⓦ www.hertz.ua ⓛ Town: 09.00–18.00 Mon–Fri; airport: 09.00–23.00

Kiev is a city of golden domes – these belong to the Caves Monastery

THE CITY OF

Kiev

Central Kiev

Kiev's small centre is where most business, politics and tourism happens. To the east lies Khreschatyk Park, which has beautiful views over the River Dnipro and contains some lovely features, including the small iron Lovers' Bridge, the Kiev Puppet Theatre, and the Summer Estrada, an open-air stage where cultural events take place in the warmer months. You can easily spend an afternoon here looking around the Water Information Centre or picnicking near the Nations Friendship Arch, a rainbow-like metal monument built in Soviet times to celebrate the reunification of Russia and Ukraine. Some of the area's best attractions, including the Mariinsky Palace and Parliament buildings, are located on the park's border. Head north from the city centre to reach Podil (see page 100), south to find the monastery area of Pechersk (see page 90), or west to get to the Central Railway Station.

SIGHTS & ATTRACTIONS

Andriivsky uzviz (Andrew's Descent)

Named after the Apostle (see page 73), this quaint cobbled street winds its way downhill from the city centre to Podil. On the way you'll pass stalls selling arts and crafts, various musicians and mime artists, some food vendors and several good art galleries. At the top is the beautiful Baroque **Andriyivska Tserkva** (St Andrew's Church 10.00–18.30 Thur–Tues Metro: Poshtova Ploscha), which was built around the 1750s by Rastrelli, architect of the Mariinsky Palace, and is now a museum. Opposite are the remains of the **Desiatynna (Tithing) Church**. Originally built in 989 as the Mother of God Church, it was destroyed during the Mongol invasion of 1240. The construction of a new church at the site has been mooted.

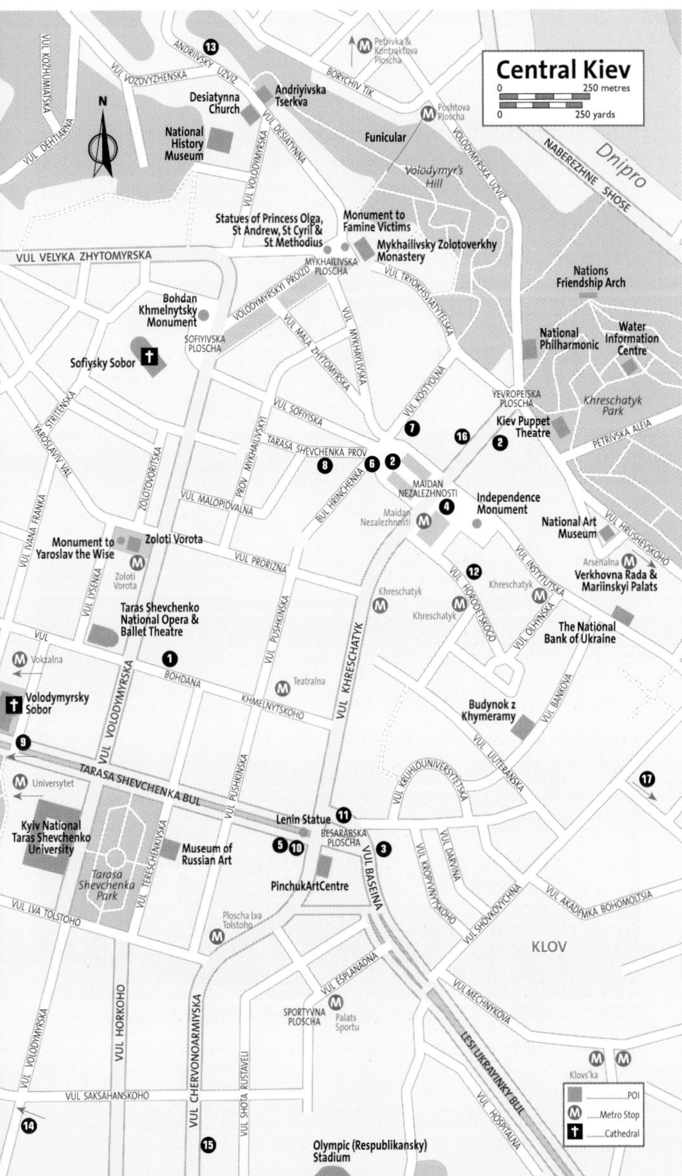

Central Kiev
0 250 metres
0 250 yards
Dnipro
Andriyivska Tserkva
Desiatynna Church
National History Museum
Funicular
Volodymyr's Hill
Statues of Princess Olga, St Andrew, St Cyril & St Methodius
Monument to Famine Victims
Mykhailivsky Zolotoverkhy Monastery
Nations Friendship Arch
Bohdan Khmelnytsky Monument
Sofiysky Sobor
National Philharmonic
Water Information Centre
Khreschatyk Park
Kiev Puppet Theatre
Independence Monument
National Art Museum
Monument to Yaroslav the Wise
Zoloti Vorota
Verkhovna Rada & Mariinskyi Palats
Taras Shevchenko National Opera & Ballet Theatre
The National Bank of Ukraine
Volodymyrsky Sobor
Budynok z Khymeramy
Lenin Statue
Kyiv National Taras Shevchenko University
Museum of Russian Art
PinchukArtCentre
Tarasa Shevchenka Park
KLOV
Olympic (Respublikansky) Stadium
Petrivka & Kontraktova Ploscha
Poshtova Ploscha
Maidan Nezalezhnosti
Zoloti Vorota
Khreschatyk
Arsenalna
Vokzalna
Teatralna
Universytet
Ploscha Lva Tolstoho
Palats Sportu
Klovs'ka
MYKHAILIVSKA PLOSCHA
SOFIYIVSKA PLOSCHA
YEVROPEISKA PLOSCHA
MAIDAN NEZALEZHNOSTI
BESARABSKA PLOSCHA
SPORTYVNA PLOSCHA
VUL KOZHUMIATSKA
VUL DEHTIARNA
VUL VOZDVYZHENSKA
ANDRIIVSKY UZVIZ
BORYCHIV TIK
VUL DESIATYNNA
VUL VOLODYMYRSKA
VOLODYMYRSKA UZVIZ
NABEREZHNE SHOSE
VUL VELYKA ZHYTOMYRSKA
VOLODYMYRSKYI PROIZD
VUL TRYOKHSVIATYTELSKA
VUL MALA ZHYTOMYRSKA
VUL MYKHAYLIVSKA
VUL KOSTYOLNA
VUL SOFIYIVSKA
TARASA SHEVCHENKA PROV
PROV MYKHAILIVSKYI
BUL HRINCHENKA
PETRIVSKA ALEIA
STRITENSKA
YAROSLAVIV VAL
ZOLOTOVORITSKA
VUL MALOPIDVALNA
VUL IVANA FRANKA
VUL PRORIZNA
VUL HRUSHEVSKOHO
VUL INSTYTUTSKA
VUL HORODETSKOGO
VUL LYSENKA
VUL PUSHKINSKA
VUL KHRESCHATYK
VUL OLHYNSKA
VUL BOHDANA KHMELNYTSKOHO
VUL BANKOVA
VUL LIUTERANSKA
VUL KRUHLOUNIVERSYTETSKA
TARASA SHEVCHENKA BUL
VUL TERESCHENKIVSKA
VUL BASEINA
VUL KROPYVNYTSKOHO
VUL DARVINA
VUL SHOVKOVYCHNA
VUL AKADEMIKA BOHOMOLTSIA
VUL LVA TOLSTOHO
VUL ESPLANADNA
VUL MECHNYKOVA
LESI UKRAYINKY BUL
VUL HORKOHO
VUL CHERVONOARMIYSKA
VUL SHOTA RUSTAVELI
VUL SAKSAHANSKOHO
VUL HOSPITALNA
POI
Metro Stop
Cathedral

St Andrew's Church marks the start of visitors' descent into Podil

THE LEGEND OF ST ANDREW

Andriivsky uzviz (Andrew's Descent) is named after St Andrew, the first disciple of Christ. A local legend has it that the Apostle sailed up the River Dnipro, landed near here, climbed the hill and planted a cross. St Andrew is also said to have predicted the formation of a great city on the site.

Budynok z Khymeramy (House with Chimeras)

The strangest building in Kiev, decorated with gargoyles and other weird animals, it was built around 1900 by architect Vladyslav Horodetsky (for more details, see page 15). Today it houses presidential offices. ⓐ Bankova 10 Ⓜ Metro: Khreschatyk

Khreschatyk

Running for nearly 2 km (1¼ miles) from European Square through Independence Square to Besarabska Square, this is one of Kiev's oldest and most important streets. Most of the buildings in the street were completely destroyed in World War II, but Khreschatyk is now lined with shops, boutiques and restaurants. During weekends, the street becomes pedestrian-only, and the local populace comes out to party.

Lenin Statue

Yes, there is one remaining statue of Lenin in Kiev. Get a picture while you can, as it may not last: its nose and hand were smashed by activists in 2009, and at its post-restoration unveiling ceremony protestors threw paint at it, prompting a melée. ⓐ Besarabska pl., at the eastern end of Tarasa Shevchenka bul. Ⓜ Metro: Ploscha Lva Tolstoho

Maidan Nezalezhnosti (Independence Square)

This urban space has become the focal point of Kiev. It gained international prominence in 2004 during the 'Orange Revolution', when it filled with citizens protesting at an improper election.

The square is filled with fountains and statues, including a bronze sculpture of the four legendary siblings who founded Kiev – brothers Kyi, Schek, Khoryv and their sister Lybid – and the newer Independence Monument, erected in 2001. Above ground, the square is active with food and souvenir stands, while in the evening people congregate to enjoy a drink while listening to street musicians; below ground is a large shopping centre. Metro: Maidan Nezalezhnosti

Even though you can't go inside, the Mariinsky Palace is well worth a visit

Mariinskyi Palats (Mariinsky Palace)

The palace was built in 1755 as a residence for royalty visiting Kiev and is named after Maria, wife of Tsar Alexander II. The beautiful blue-and-cream coloured building was designed in a Russian Baroque style, similar to that of the Summer Palace in St Petersburg. The building is closed to the public and used mainly for special occasions by the Ukrainian president. However, the nearby Khreschatyk Park is beautiful and worth a walk around. ⓐ Hrushevskoho 5 Ⓜ Metro: Arsenalna

Mykhailivsky Zolotoverkhy Monastery (St Michael's Golden-Domed Monastery)

Named after Kiev's patron saint, this monastery was originally built in 1108 but was destroyed by the Soviets in 1936. After independence

it was rebuilt and it opened in 2001. It features medieval/Baroque styling, with seven bright golden domes. On the square surrounding the monastery is a monument to the five million victims of the great famines of 1932 and 1933. Also on the square are statues of St Andrew, Princess Olga and the Byzantine Saints Cyril and Methodius, who invented the Cyrillic alphabet and brought literacy to the Slav peoples. ⓐ Mykhailivska pl. ⓣ 279 2248 ◷ 08.00–19.00 or 20.00; services: 08.00 & 17.00 Mon–Sat, 08.00, 10.00 & 17.00 Sun Ⓜ Metro: Maidan Nezalezhnosti

Sofiysky Sobor (St Sophia's Cathedral)

Kiev's oldest church was completed in 1037. Inside are mosaics and other artwork dating back to the time of construction. The church's Byzantine architecture derives from that of Constantinople (Istanbul), capital of the Eastern Orthodox Church at the time. The most important mosaic is the *Virgin Orans*, which has great significance to the Orthodox religion. The Cathedral is a UNESCO World Heritage site. ⓐ Volodymyrska 24 ⓣ 279 2256 ◷ 10.00–18.00 Thur–Tues, 10.00–17.00 Wed Ⓜ Metro: Maidan Nezalezhnosti or Zoloti Vorota ⓘ Admission charge

Verkhovna Rada (National Parliament)

This building and the Mariinsky Palace form one site. The members of the Ukrainian Parliament meet beneath its glass dome, and it was here on 24 August 1991 that Ukrainian independence was declared. The building is not open to visitors. Ⓜ Metro: Arsenalna

Volodymyrsky Sobor (St Volodymyr's Cathedral)

This is one of Kiev's newer churches, started in 1862 and completed in 1892. It is probably the most highly decorated church in the city, and its grand opening was attended by Tsar Nicholas II. It was built in Byzantine style, with a bright yellow exterior and seven blue domes sporting gilded stars. The artwork inside is awesome, with large paintings on the walls and ceilings depicting the spiritual history of Kiev. This is a church still much used by the people of Kiev, so if you want to see an Orthodox service, this is the place to go. Tarasa Shevchenka bul. 20 235 5385, 235 0362 06.00–19.30; services: 08.00 & 17.00 Mon–Fri, 07.00, 10.00 & 17.00 Sat & Sun Metro: Universytet

Zoloti Vorota (Golden Gate)

This is a replica of the main entrance to Kiev, which was originally erected in 1037 to protect the city. It was destroyed in the Mongol invasion of 1240 and this reconstruction was completed in 1982. Nearby stands a monument to Yaroslav the Wise, a national hero who built St Sophia's Cathedral, founded the first library in the medieval state of Kyivan Rus and compiled its first legal code, which was used for the next 400 years. Volodymyrska at Yaroslaviv Val 10.00–18.00 Fri–Tues Metro: Zoloti Vorota Admission charge

CULTURE

Museum of Russian Art

This small but luxurious mansion houses Kiev's greatest collection of Russian art. An important piece is the icon of St George slaying the dragon. The building also gives an idea of the lifestyle of the wealthy in pre-Russian Revolution days. Tereschenkivska 9 234 6218 11.00–18.00 Mon, 10.00–18.00 Tues, Fri & Sun, 12.00–20.00 Sat; closed last Mon of the month Metro: Ploscha Lva Tolstoho Admission charge

National Art Museum

Built in the late 19th century in the style of a Greek temple, with six large columns forming the portico, its collection is largely unknown to the Western world. The works are mainly by Ukrainian artists and include icons, paintings and sculptures from the 14th to 20th centuries. ⓐ Hrushevskoho 6 ⓣ 278 1357 ⓦ www.namu.kiev.ua ◷ 10.00–18.00 Wed, Thur & Sun, 12.00–19.00 Fri, 11.00–19.00 Sat Ⓜ Metro: Maidan Nezalezhnosti ⓘ Admission charge

National History Museum

The museum covers Ukrainian history from prehistoric times up to the present. The collections include art, archaeological artefacts, old books and coins. The museum is located near St Andrew's Church and the Desiatynna Church ruins. ⓐ Volodymyrska 2 ⓣ 278 4864 ◷ 10.00–17.00 Thur–Tues Ⓜ Metro: Poshtova Ploscha ⓘ Admission charge

PinchukArtCentre (Museum of Contemporary Art)

The biggest contemporary art centre not just in Ukraine but in Eastern Europe, with a busy programme of exhibitions, cultural projects and workshops. ⓐ Arena Complex, Chervonoarmiyska 1–3 ⓣ 590 0858 ⓦ www.pinchukartcentre.org ◷ 12.00–21.00 Tues–Sun Ⓜ Metro: Ploscha Lva Tolstoho

Taras Shevchenko National Opera & Ballet Theatre

The building is lavish, both inside and out, and the performances are never less than grandiose. Completed in 1901 and designed in Viennese style, it is one of the best-preserved buildings in the city. It is also the site of the assassination of Pyotr Stolypin, the prime minister of Tsar Nicholas II, in 1911, part of an abortive attempt

Zoloti Vorota is a reconstruction of the legendary Golden Gate of Kiev

to reform the government. The only way to see the inside is to take in one of the performances, but that's a good idea anyway.
ⓐ Volodymyrska 50 ⓣ 234 7165; box office: 279 1169 ⓦ www.opera.com.ua Ⓝ Metro: Zoloti Vorota or Teatralna ⓘ Admission charge

Kiev has some impressive shopping centres

RETAIL THERAPY

Alta Centre This mall has a complete range of products for sale, from clothing and shoes to sportswear, cosmetics and souvenirs. There are two department stores, a supermarket and several restaurants on site. Fashion Lab is a unique collection of boutiques featuring Ukrainian designs. On most Saturdays (except in summer) there is a show of the latest Ukrainian trends. ⓐ Moskovsky prosp. 11A ⓣ 426 5454 ⓛ 10.00–22.00 ⓜ Metro: Petrivka

Atelier Karas A commercial art gallery that features contemporary works by local artists. ⓐ Andriivsky uzviz 22A ⓣ 238 6531 ⓛ 10.00–18.00 ⓜ Metro: Kontraktova Ploscha

Besarabsky Rynok Also known as the Bessarabian Market, this is the place to buy the best quality fruit, vegetables and other foodstuffs. It is a farmers' market, and worth visiting just to see how the locals shop for their daily diet. You can get free samples of many of the products. Sadly, most of the fruit and vegetables are now imported, with high prices. To find a true Ukrainian market, you will have to travel further outside the city. ⓐ Besarabska pl. 2 ⓛ 08.00–17.00 Mon, 08.00–20.00 Tues–Sun ⓜ Metro: Khreschatyk

Globus Located at the underground shopping centre at Maidan Nezalezhnosti, the shops here sell clothing, shoes, lingerie and accessories. Many designer labels, such as Esprit, Polo and Hilfiger, are represented. It is one of the best places to buy clothes in Kiev. ⓐ Maidan Nezalezhnosti ⓣ 371 1137 ⓦ www.globus.com.ua ⓛ 10.00–22.00 ⓜ Metro: Maidan Nezalezhnosti

Khreschatyk This thoroughfare (see page 73) and the ones nearby seem to be doing a rather good impression of London's Oxford Street these days. The international, big-name stores have piled in alongside all the local shops that were already there. The latter are the ones that attract visitors first, with their quality jewellery, antiques and folk art. Fast-food outlets, cafés and bars also line the street and add to the vibe. Metro: Khreschatyk or Maidan Nezalezhnosti

Mandarin Plaza A seven-storey shopping centre with a full range of outlets, the plaza is very smart – this is where the wealthy locals shop. Baseina 6 230 9590 www.mandarin.kiev.ua 10.00–22.00 Metro: Ploscha Lva Tolstoho

Metrograd Underground Shopping Complex Another underground shopping centre where you can buy just about anything. Under Besarabska pl. & Velyka Vasylkivska 247 5665 www.metrograd.com 09.00–21.00 Metro: Ploscha Lva Tolstoho

TsUM (Central Universal Shop) TsUM is an old, Russian-style department store, housed in a monolithic building. It is moving upmarket, but is still the best place to go to buy the basics. Bohdana Khmelnytskoho 2 234 9505 10.00–20.00 Mon–Fri, 11.00–20.00 Sat, 11.00–19.00 Sun Metro: Khreschatyk or Teatralna

Ukraina Shopping Mall This centre has five floors for shopping, a cinema, a bowling club, a pharmacy, a bookshop and a 24-hour supermarket. Peremohy prosp. 3 496 1627 Mall: 10.00–21.00; supermarket (separate entrance): 24 hrs Metro: Vokzalna

TAKING A BREAK

Domashnya Kukhnya (Home Cooking) £ ❶ This place serves a great variety of Ukrainian food, along with hot and cold drinks. It is cafeteria-style, but the quality is good and the prices are low, and as a result it becomes noisy and crowded at main mealtimes and at weekends. ⓐ Bohdana Khmelnytskoho 16–22 ⓣ 234 2918 ⓒ 08.00–23.00 ⓜ Metro: Teatralna

Dva Gusya (Two Geese) £ ❷ Part of a local fast-food chain. In Maidan you can choose between the underground food court in the Globus shopping centre and the restaurant on the first floor of a nearby building on Khreschatyk. All traditional local fare with low prices and good quality. ⓐ Khreschatyk 7–11 or Globus (see page 81) ⓣ 279 8904 ⓦ www.dvagusya.ua ⓒ 09.00–23.00 ⓜ Metro: Maidan Nezalezhnosti

Puzata Hata (Paunchy House) £ ❸ Take the name of this reaturant seriously: it will send the calorie count sky-high. Housed in an authentic peasant house, the lower floor serves main courses, while the second floor specialises in pastries. Breakfast, lunch and dinner are served, and there's authentic Ukrainian food at low prices. There are eight other outlets around the city. ⓐ Baseina 2A ⓣ 391 4699 ⓦ www.puzatahata.com.ua ⓒ 07.30–23.00 ⓜ Metro: Ploscha Lva Tolstoho

Shvydko £ ❹ Kiev's version of McDonald's. Fast food, *borsch*, *varenyky*, chicken Kiev and salads are staples, and there is a children's menu. ⓐ Maidan Nezalezhnosti ⓣ 278 6362 ⓒ 07.00–23.00 ⓜ Metro: Maidan Nezalezhnosti

Antresol ££ ❺ This is a combination coffee house and bookshop. The menu includes cakes, pastries, fruit cocktails and other desserts. The books are in English, Russian and Ukrainian. There is an exchange system that allows you to trade in your old books for new ones, or even for coffee and food. ⓐ Tarasa Shevchenka bul. 2 ⓣ 235 8347 ◷ 08.00–24.00 Ⓜ Metro: Ploscha Lva Tolstoho

Coffee Time ££ ❻ A popular coffee shop offering one of the most varied choices of hot and cold drinks, snacks and cakes in Kiev – even better, it's open 24 hours. ⓐ Borysa Hrinchenka 2/1 ⓣ 278 2156 ◷ 24 hrs Ⓜ Metro: Maidan Nezalezhnosti

Coffeeum in Maidan ££ ❼ No shy and retiring, demure spot but a big and bold joint on two floors where you can have a coffee, a cigar and a cognac in any order you like. There's an enclosure for VIPs called the 'Old Piano'. ⓐ Kostyolna 4 ⓣ 278 0490 ◷ 08.00–24.00 Ⓜ Metro: Maidan Nezalezhnosti

Kaffa ££ ❽ A smoke-free café, which is rare in Kiev, Kaffa serves a wide variety of very tasty coffees. The menu is long, and the service good but slow. The interior is decorated in an African motif, with masks, beads and leather. ⓐ Tarasa Shevchenka prov. 3 ⓣ 270 6505 ◷ 09.00–23.00 Mon–Fri, 10.00–23.00 Sat & Sun Ⓜ Metro: Maidan Nezalezhnosti

Repriza ££ ❾ With a long tradition catering to the sweet tooth of Kiev consumers, this patisserie channels a Viennese vibe. As well as a gamut of cakes, pastries, posh chocolates and other sugary goodies, there are also some savoury eats such as soups, sandwiches and salads. Other outlets can be found at Sahaidachnoho 10/5,

Velyka Zhytomyrska 38, Chervonoarmiyska 26 and Lva Tolstoho 11/61. ⓐ Khmelnytskoho 40/25 ⓣ 502 2346 ⓦ www.repriza.com ◷ 08.00–22.00 ⓜ Metro: Universytet

Viola's Bierstube £££ ❿ One for the health-food freaks. Located near the Lenin Statue, it serves salads, juices and other healthy food containing the kinds of vitamins and minerals we should be eating. It also offers a variety of low-calorie desserts. ⓐ Tarasa Shevchenka bul. 1 ⓣ 235 3751 ◷ 11.00–02.00 ⓜ Metro: Ploscha Lva Tolstoho

AFTER DARK

RESTAURANTS

TGI Friday's ££ ⓫ Don't groan – TGI Friday's may be an international chain but it's dearly loved by Ukrainian locals for its large portions, reasonable prices and excellent service. It's a good choice if you have children. ⓐ Besarabska pl. 5A ⓣ 235 4264 ⓦ www.fridays.com.ua ◷ 12.00–23.00 ⓜ Metro: Ploscha Lva Tolstoho

Fellini ££–£££ ⓬ Located near Maidan, this cinema-themed restaurant serves a mixture of French and Italian dishes. ⓐ Horodetskogo 5 ⓣ 279 5462 ◷ 24 hrs ⓜ Metro: Maidan Nezalezhnosti

Za Dvoma Zaytsamy ££–£££ ⓭ The restaurant is named after a cult film of the same name, based on a Ukrainian proverb that says if you chase two hares, you will catch neither. The décor is 19th century, the food is authentic and reasonably priced, and the menu, of course, includes some rabbit dishes. ⓐ Andriivsky uzviz 34 ⓣ 279 7972 ◷ 11.00–23.00 ⓜ Metro: Kontraktova Ploscha

The Independence Monument dominates Maidan Nezalezhnosti by night

Lavinia £££ ⓮ Located next to the biggest wine merchant in Kiev, this restaurant boasts the best wine list in the city. ⓐ Zhylianska 59 ⓣ 569 5700 ⓛ 10.00–23.00 ⓝ Metro: Universytet

Vagon Restaurant £££ ⓯ The name means 'Carriage Restaurant' and it is styled accordingly. Enjoy your meal in train compartments that never move. ⓐ Chervonoarmiyska (Velyka Vasylkivska) 52 ⓣ 287 0490 ⓛ 13.00–01.00 ⓝ Metro: Ploscha Lva Tolstoho

Buddha-bar £££–££££ ⓰ The trendiest establishment in Kiev, this Asian restaurant serves Indian, Chinese, Japanese and Thai dishes with a European twist. ⓐ Khreschatyk 14 ⓣ 270 7676 ⓦ www.buddhabar.com.ua ⓛ 13.00–02.00 Mon–Thur, 13.00–04.00 Fri & Sat, 14.00–02.00 Sun ⓝ Metro: Khreschatyk

Lypsky Osobnyak £££–££££ ⓱ This place is reputed to serve the finest Ukrainian food in the city. This is another restaurant featuring fine 19th-century décor, and it offers excellent service and a large wine cellar. ⓐ Lypska 15 ⓣ 254 0090 ⓛ 11.30–01.00 ⓝ Metro: Arsenalna

BARS & CLUBS

Arena The most central and modern venue in Kiev. ⓐ Baseina 2A ⓣ 492 0000 ⓦ www.arena-kiev.com ⓛ 22.00–06.00 Tues–Sun ⓝ Metro: Ploscha Lva Tolstoho

Art Club 44 Primarily a cellar jazz club, but other music is played. It is unpretentious and usually crowded. There is a cover charge, and drinks are expensive. ⓐ Kreshchatyk 44 ⓣ 279 4137 ⓦ www.club44.com.ua ⓛ 11.00–23.00 Sun–Thur, 11.00–04.00 Fri & Sat ⓝ Metro: Teatralna

Bierstube German-style beer hall located in a basement, catering for wealthier clients. The beer is good but pricey. ⓐ Chervonoarmiyska 20 ⓣ 235 9472 ◷ 08.00–02.00 ⓜ Metro: Ploscha Lva Tolsovo

Golden Gate Irish Pub Typical Irish bar featuring great pub food, draught beer and Irish whiskey. ⓐ Zolotovoritska 15 ⓣ 235 5188 ⓦ www.goldengatepubkiev.com ◷ 10.00–late ⓜ Metro: Zoloti Vorota

O'Brien's Irish Pub This is the place to have a good time with expats. Reputed to have no class and cheap bands, but it is still a good meeting place. ⓐ Mykhaylivska 17A ⓣ 279 1584 ⓦ www.obriens.kiev.ua ◷ 08.00–02.00 ⓜ Metro: Maidan Nezalezhnosti

CLASSICAL MUSIC & THEATRE

Almost all performances are in Ukrainian or Russian, with the exception of opera, which are performed in their original languages. However, it is worth attending a performance to see the lavish costumes and scenery, and to feel the reaction of the audience.

House of Organ and Chamber Music Hosts classical concerts inside the century-old, Gothic-style St Nicholas Cathedral. ⓐ Chervonoarmiyska (Velyka Vasylkivska) 77 ⓣ 528 3186 ⓜ Metro: Respublikansky Stadion

National Philharmonic Ukraine's National Symphonic Orchestra takes part in concerts and festivals. Its home is a beautiful building that was once the headquarters of the Kiev Merchants' Assembly. ⓐ Volodymyrsky uzviz 2 ⓣ 278 1697 ⓦ www.filarmonia.com.ua ⓜ Metro: Maidan Nezalezhnosti

Palace of Sports Although primarily used for sporting events, this is also a regular venue for rock and pop concerts. Sportyvna pl. 1 246 7406 Metro: Palats Sportu

Taras Shevchenko National Opera & Ballet Theatre No trip to Kiev would be complete without attending a performance at the Opera House. The productions are second to none, and the venue is also world class (see page 78). Even if this kind of entertainment is not your thing, it is still an enjoyable Ukrainian experience. There are performances just about every night starting at about 19.00, as well as matinées on many days at 12.00. Prices are low, starting at around 20hr., but you may want to pay more in order to get good seats. Volodymyrska 50 234 7165; box office: 279 1169 www.opera.com.ua Metro: Zoloti Vorota or Teatralna

CINEMAS

There are currently only a handful of cinemas in central Kiev that show films in their original English; however, the number is growing. A monthly cinema club and frequent film festivals also provide a steady flow of films that are shown in their original language.

Kyiv Chervonoarmiyska (Velyka Vasylkivska) 19 234 7381 Metro: Ploscha Lva Tolstoho

Odessa Peremohy prosp. 3 496 1511 Metro: Vokzalna

Pechersk

Pechersk means 'of the caves', and is the old, historic heart of Kiev. The building of the caves started in 1051 and the construction of the first surface building followed shortly after. The area developed to make Kiev the cultural and spiritual centre of Slavic Christianity from ancient times up to the Russian Revolution.

SIGHTS & ATTRACTIONS

Kievo-Pecherska Lavra (The Caves Monastery)
Kiev's top tourist attraction is in fact many attractions in one. Besides the caves, there are several museums and many churches. There is a general admission charge to the Upper Lavra site, and then individual entrance fees to most of the churches and museums, as well as an extra charge if you want to take pictures. This can add up, so you may want to consider taking a guided tour, or even hiring a personal guide. Admission to the Lower Lavra and caves themselves is free, which the guides are reluctant to tell you. Note that the caves are sometimes closed for maintenance.

Although the site is officially a government-owned Historical and Cultural Preserve – with the exception of the Lower Lavra and the caves themselves, which belong to the church – it is also a religious shrine of the Ukrainian Orthodox Church, under the authority of the Moscow Patriarch. Every year tens of thousands of devout Orthodox Christians make a pilgrimage to pray at the Lavra, considered the spiritual heart of the country. Visitors should treat this as a very holy site, and act with the appropriate reverence and respect. Unfortunately, souvenir shops and other devices to separate visitors from their money are starting to pervade the site.

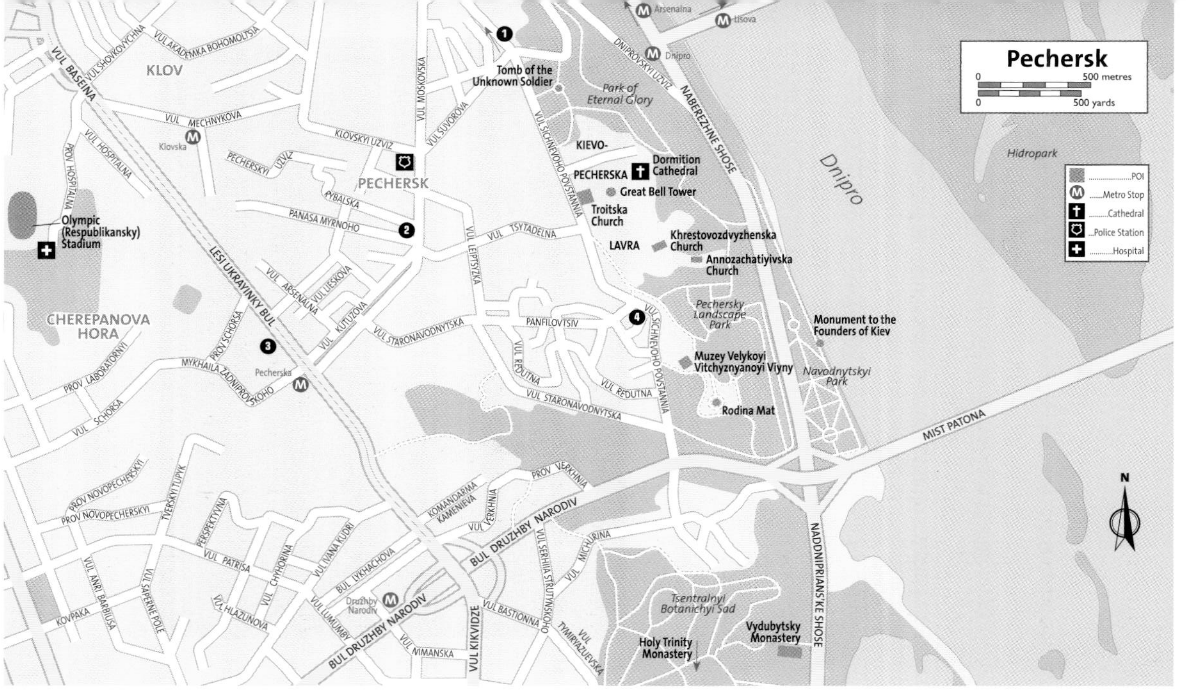

Pechersk
0
500 metres
0
500 yards
POI
Metro Stop
Cathedral
Police Station
Hospital
N
Hidropark
Dnipro
Arsenalna
Lisova
Dnipro
DNIPROVSKYI UZVIZ
NABEREZHNE SHOSE
Tomb of the Unknown Soldier
Park of Eternal Glory
KIEVO-
PECHERSKA
Dormition Cathedral
Great Bell Tower
Troitska Church
LAVRA
Khrestovozdvyzhenska Church
Annozachatiyivska Church
Pechersky Landscape Park
Monument to the Founders of Kiev
Muzey Velykoyi Vitchyznyanoyi Viyny
Navodnytskyi Park
Rodina Mat
MIST PATONA
NADDNIPRIANS'KE SHOSE
Tsentralnyi Botanichyi Sad
Vydubytsky Monastery
Holy Trinity Monastery
KLOV
VUL SHOVKOVYCHNA
VUL AKADEMKA BOHOMOLTSIA
VUL BASEINA
VUL MECHNYKOVA
Klovska
VUL MOSKOVSKA
VUL SUVOROVA
KLOVSKYI UZVIZ
PECHERSKYI UZVIZ
PECHERSK
RYBALSKA
PANASA MYRNOHO
VUL SICHNEVOHO POVSTANNIA
VUL TSYTADELNA
VUL LEIPTSYZKA
PROV HOSPITALNA
VUL HOSPITALNA
Olympic (Respublikansky) Stadium
LESI UKRAYINKY BUL
VUL ARSENALNA
VUL LIESKOVA
VUL KUTUZOVA
VUL STARONAVODNYTSKA
PANFILOVTSIV
VUL REDUTNA
CHEREPANOVA HORA
PROV SCHORSA
Pecherska
MYKHAILA ZADNIPROVSKOHO
PROV LABORATORNYI
VUL SCHORSA
PROV VERKHNIA
KOMANDARMA KAMENIEVA
VUL VERKHNIA
BUL DRUZHBY NARODIV
VUL MICHURINA
VUL SERHIIA STRUTYNSKOHO
PROV NOVOPECHERSKYI
PROV NOVOPECHERSKYI
TVERSKYI TUPYK
PERSPEKTYVNA
VUL IVANA KUDRI
BUL LYKHACHOVA
VUL PATRISA
VUL CHYHORINA
VUL ANRI BARBIUSA
VUL SAPERNE POLE
VUL HLAZUNOVA
KOVPAKA
VUL LUMUMBY
Druzhby Narodiv
VUL NIMANSKA
VUL KIKVIDZE
VUL BASTIONNA
VUL TYMIRYAZUEVSKA

Visiting the caves is a very moving experience, even for the non-believer. However, if you are claustrophobic, do not even think of entering, as the caves are barely 2 m (6½ ft) high, and less than 1 m (3 ft) wide. Although the entrance is free, you may want to pay for a guided tour, as they do not make it easy for an independent traveller to find the exact entrance spot. It is customary to purchase a candle when entering, and, as the cost is only a few hryvnia, you should do so. Photography is not allowed, talking should only be done in whispers, women are expected to cover their heads, and men are required to remove their hats. Due to the popularity of the site, try to avoid weekends, or, if you can only visit at a weekend, go early. Many sections of the caves are now blocked off and reserved for the use of monks and true pilgrims only.

A lit shrine gleams in the caves

THE HISTORY OF THE CAVES MONASTERY

A Lavra is a major monastery of the Eastern (Orthodox) Church, headed by an archimandrite – the equivalent of an abbot in Western denominations. The Kyivan Lavra was founded by the Russian monk later to be known as St Anthony of the Caves, who had taken his vows at the famous monastery of Athos in Greece, in the mid-11th century.

The cave he occupied had previously been inhabited by Ilarion, who later became the first Metropolitan of Kiev. The first monks excavated more caves and built a church above them. The monastery attracted powerful and wealthy patrons, and soon became the largest religious and cultural centre in what is now Ukraine.

The monastery was a target for envious invaders, including the Mongols and the Tatars, and was sacked and destroyed several times, but arose again on each occasion. It became an important educational and cultural centre, and in the 17th century housed the first printing press in Ukraine.

Repression continued, first by the imperial authorities of Russia (who confiscated the enormous property – including three cities and seven towns – owned by the monastery as a result of gifts from its patrons) and later by the Soviets, who seized most of the relics and precious artefacts and attempted to turn the site into a centre for anti-religious propaganda. In 1941, retreating Russian forces blew up the Dormition Cathedral as the German army entered Kiev.

After World War II, the Soviet authorities allowed the reinstitution of the Lavra and the site was restored.

The Near Caves were started by St Anthony, who as a hermit did not take to the communal life of the main monastery he had helped to found in the original (Far) caves. He is buried here, as are over 120 other monks. There are three churches in the Near Caves, including the Vvedenska Church, famous for its gold icons. The entrance is through the Khrestovozdvyzhenska Church (Church of the Raising of the Cross), built in 1700.

The Far Caves entrance is connected to the Near Caves exit by a covered walkway. The Far Caves also have three underground churches, as well as the remains of many mummified monks. The entrance is in the Annozachatiyivska Church (Church of the Conception of St Anna), built in 1679.

The Troitska Church (Gate Church of the Trinity) is now used as the main entrance to the Lavra. It was built in 1108, and features interesting murals, painted in 1900, on its outside walls. The Great Bell Tower is nearly 100 m (300 ft) tall – the world's tallest Orthodox building. If you want a panoramic view of the Lavra, and most of Kiev, you can climb the nearly 200 steps to the top. Be careful, as the steps and guardrail are not as safe as they should be.

The Dormition (Uspenskyi) Cathedral, or Church of the Assumption, was originally built in 1077, and is technically the oldest above-ground church in the Lavra. The original was destroyed in World War II, but rebuilt by the city of Kiev in 1998–2000. It features seven beautiful gold domes, and is the resting place of St Theodosius.

There are many other religious sites at the Lavra, including the Church of All Saints (Tserkva Vsikh Sviatykh), the Chapel of St Anthony and St Theodosius, the St Nicholas Church (Tserkva Sviatoho Mykolaya), the Refectory, the monks' dormitories, the Church of the Nativity of the Virgin (1696), and the Bell Tower of the Far Caves (1761). ⓐ Ivana Mazepy (Sichnevoho Povstannia) 21 ⓣ 280 3071 ⓦ www.kplavra.kiev.ua

The magnificent Dormition (Uspenskyi) Cathedral

09.00–19.00 summer; 09.30–18.00 winter (last entry one hour before closing) Metro: Arsenalna, then bus 24 or trolleybus 38 Admission charge

Rodina Mat at the Museum of the Great Patriotic War

Muzey Velykoyi Vitchyznyanoyi Viyny (Museum of the Great Patriotic War)

This is located just south of the Caves Monastery. It is a memorial complex dedicated to the Ukrainian struggle against the Nazis in World War II. The panoramas and exhibits are quite sobering. The focal point of the museum is a 62-m (203-ft)-high statue of a female warrior called Rodina Mat ('the Nation's Mother'). Referred to as the 'Iron Maiden', she is actually built of titanium. It is possible to take an elevator or stairs up to her right hand, where there is a viewing platform. In the park surrounding the museum there is statuary, an Eternal Flame, displays of military equipment and, at the northern end, the Tomb of the Unknown Soldier. Ⓐ Ivana Mazepy (Sichnevoho Povstannia) 44 Ⓣ 285 9452 Ⓦ www.warmuseum.kiev.ua 🕒 10.00–17.00 Tues–Sun Ⓜ Metro: Arsenalna, then bus 24 or trolleybus 38 ⓘ Admission charge

Tsentralnyi Botanichyi Sad (Central Botanic Gardens)

This park lies along the banks of the River Dnipro and was opened in 1936. It features over 13,000 trees, bushes and other plants from five continents. It was once owned by the nearby Vydubytsky Monastery (see below), and there are spectacular views of the gardens and river from the monastery. Ⓐ Tymiryazievska 1 Ⓣ 285 4105 Ⓦ www.nbg.kiev.ua 🕒 08.30–21.00 (closes dusk in winter) Ⓜ Metro: Druzhby Narodiv ⓘ Admission charge

Vydubytsky Monastery

The monastery was founded in the 10th century, with St Michael's Church being built in 1070. Legend has it that after Prince Volodymyr made Kiev Christian, he cut down the pagan idol, Perun, and tossed it into the river, where it should have sunk. It did not, and at the spot where it floated ashore the monastery was established. The monastery is located at the narrowest part of the river, and for years controlled the ferry crossing here. This monastery was also the site of much of the early writing on the history of Russia and Ukraine. Although

Vydubytsky Monastery has a 1,000-year history

much of the monastery was destroyed by the Soviet regime, some of the early mosaics, frescoes and architectural features still exist. It was re-established in 1998. ⓐ Tymiryazievska 1 Ⓜ Metro: Druzhby Narodiv or from Pecherska bus 62 to the end stop

TAKING A BREAK

Coffeeum in Pechersk ££ ❶ Photos line the walls of this two-level coffee house near the Caves Monastery. ⓐ Ivana Mazepy (Sichnevoho Povstannia) 3A ⓣ 280 5796 ◷ 08.00–22.00 Ⓜ Metro: Arsenalna

AFTER DARK

RESTAURANTS

Egoist £££ ❷ This fine restaurant that serves Ukrainian and European cuisine offers cocktails and culinary hedonism alongside alcoholic connoisseurship. ⓐ Moskovska 44 ⓣ 254 2214 ⓦ www.egoist.com.ua ◷ 10.00–late Ⓜ Metro: Arsenalna

Marokana Fashion Café £££ ❸ Serving international cuisine with an oriental twist, this place caters to Kiev's wealthier set. ⓐ Lesi Ukrayinky bul. 24 ⓣ 254 4999 ⓦ http://carteblanche.com.ua ◷ 09.00–last customer Ⓜ Metro: Pecherska

Tsarske Selo Restaurant £££ ❹ Get a taste of Ukrainian village life in this themed restaurant, where staff preserve historical traditions of service and dishes are prepared to ancient recipes. ⓐ Ivana Mazepy (Sichnevoho Povstannia) 42/1 ⓣ 288 9775 ⓦ www.tsarske.kiev.ua ◷ 11.00–01.00 Ⓜ Metro: Arsenalna, then bus 24 or trolleybus 38

Podil

Podil was originally the river port of Kiev, and the place where the craftsmen and foreign merchants lived. It is on the River Dnipro plain, looking up at the rest of the city, which sits on the hills above. The area was destroyed by fire in 1811 but subsequently rebuilt. Amazingly, Podil survived the Soviet repression and World War II intact, so that the area still looks much as it did in the 19th century. In addition to the specific attractions listed below, the whole area is worth visiting for its historic buildings, small churches, synagogue and old merchants' homes. Today it is becoming gentrified as young professionals move in, and it has many boutiques and fine restaurants.

SIGHTS & ATTRACTIONS

Funicular

Connecting Podil with the city centre, this provides an alternative route to Podil from the one via Andrew's Descent (see page 70). The view is good, and the cost is only 1.50hr. You should consider walking down Andrew's Descent, exploring the streets of Podil, and then taking the funicular back up the hill to the city centre. The bottom end of the funicular is near the boat terminal, while the top end is behind St Michael's Monastery (see page 75).
06.30–23.00 Metro: Poshtova Ploscha

Kontraktova ploscha (Contract Square)

This is the very centre of Podil, an ancient marketplace where trade fairs took place in the Middle Ages. On one side is the Hostiny Dvir (Hospice Court), and on the other is the Contract House, formerly the offices for the marketplace. Metro: Kontraktova Ploscha

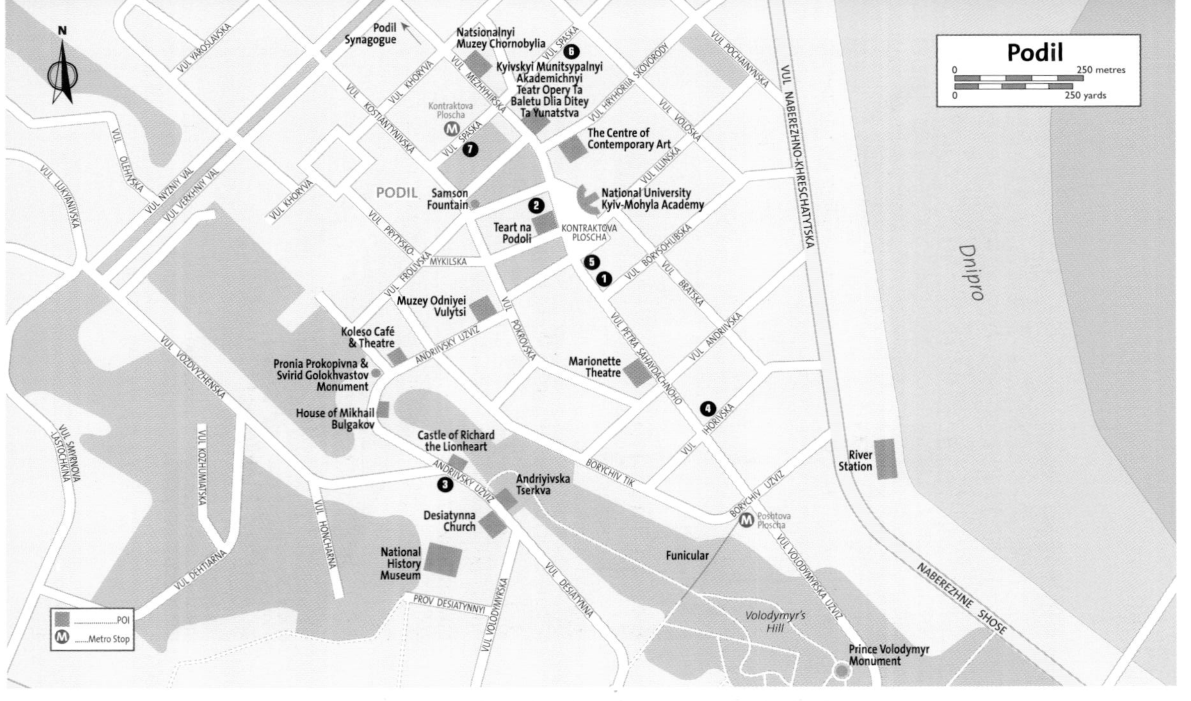
Podil
0
250 metres
0
250 yards
N
Podil Synagogue
Natsionalnyi Muzey Chornobylia
Kyivskyi Munitsypalnyi Akademichnyi Teatr Opery Ta Baletu Dlia Ditey Ta Yunatstva
The Centre of Contemporary Art
National University Kyiv-Mohyla Academy
Kontraktova Ploscha
KONTRAKTOVA PLOSCHA
PODIL
Samson Fountain
Teart na Podoli
Muzey Odniyei Vulytsi
Koleso Café & Theatre
Pronia Prokopivna & Svirid Golokhvastov Monument
House of Mikhail Bulgakov
Castle of Richard the Lionheart
Andriyivska Tserkva
Desiatynna Church
National History Museum
Marionette Theatre
River Station
Funicular
Poshtova Ploscha
Volodymyr's Hill
Prince Volodymyr Monument
Dnipro
VUL YAROSLAVSKA
VUL KHORYVA
VUL KOSTIANTYNIVSKA
VUL MEZHYHIRSKA
VUL SPASKA
VUL HRYHORIIA SKOVORODY
VUL POCHAINYNSKA
VUL VOLOSKA
VUL ILLINSKA
VUL NABEREZHNO-KHRESCHATYTSKA
VUL OLEHIVSKA
VUL NYZHNIY VAL
VUL VERKHNIY VAL
VUL LUKYANIVSKA
VUL PRYTYSKO-MYKILSKA
VUL FROLIVSKA
VUL BORYSOHLIBSKA
VUL BRATSKA
VUL ANDRIIVSKA
VUL POKROVSKA
ANDRIIVSKY UZVIZ
VUL PETRA SAHAYDACHNOHO
VUL IHORIVSKA
BORYCHIV TIK
BORYCHIV UZVIZ
VUL VOZDVYZHENSKA
VUL SMYRNOVA-LASTOCHKINA
VUL KOZHUMIATSKA
VUL HONCHARNA
VUL DEHTIARNA
PROV DESIATYNNYI
VUL VOLODYMYRSKA
VUL DESIATYNNA
VUL VOLODYMYRSKA UZVIZ
NABEREZHNE SHOSE
POI
Metro Stop

The funicular is an easy way of getting back up to the city centre

Natsionalnyi Muzey Chornobylia (National Museum of Chernobyl)
You almost feel that you are at the site of the disaster caused by the explosion of the Number 4 nuclear reactor in April 1986 (see page 110). Road signs from towns and villages near Chernobyl are used, as are old computers and other exhibits with 'don't touch' signs. Many of the exhibits are graphic and haunting, and may be scary for children. The most emotional is the film of the firemen who went in to clean up just after the accident, most of whom died within weeks due to radiation poisoning. The museum was opened in 1993 in the back of the Regional Department of Emergency Situations building on Mezhyhirska, but has few visitors. English-speaking guides are available. ⓐ Khoryva prov. 1, off Mezhyhirska ⓣ 417 5422 ⓦ www.chornobylmuseum.kiev.ua ⓑ 10.00–18.00 Mon–Fri, 10.00–17.00 Sat ⓜ Metro: Kontraktova Ploscha ⓘ Admission charge

CULTURE

Kyivskyi Munitsypalnyi Akademichnyi Teatr Opery Ta Baletu Dlia Ditey Ta Yunatstva (Kiev Municipal Academic Opera & Ballet Theatre for Youth)
One of the most interesting theatres in Kiev. Targeting a young audience, the theatre stages a wide range of shows with a live orchestra. ⓐ Mezhyhirska 2 ⓣ 425 3015 ⓜ Metro: Kontraktova Ploscha

Teart na Podoli (Podil Drama Theatre)
This theatre performs everything from light local works to Shakespeare, and the performances are generally very entertaining. ⓐ Kontraktova pl. 4 (second stage at Andriivsky uzviz 20B) ⓣ 425 0194 ⓦ www.theatreonpodol.com ⓜ Metro: Kontraktova Ploscha

MUSEUM OF ONE STREET

Muzey Odniyei Vulytsi, or the Museum of One Street, is at the bottom of Andrew's Descent and covers this street's history from before the Russian Revolution to the present day. Its collection of simple artefacts, such as cloths, eyeglasses, dishes and books, is displayed in such a way that you get a real feel for how people actually lived here. ⓐ Andriivsky uzviz 2B ⓣ 425 0398 ⓦ www.onestreet.kiev.ua ◷ 12.00–18.00 Tues–Sun ⓝ Metro: Kontraktova Ploscha ⓘ Admission charge

TAKING A BREAK

Puzata Hata £ ❶ The Podil branch of this establishment is very similar to that in the city centre (see page 83) – good Ukrainian food, if a trifle noisy. ⓐ Sahaydachnoho 24 ⓣ 391 4699 ⓦ www.puzata hata.com.ua ◷ 08.00–23.00 ⓝ Metro: Kontraktova Ploscha

Piano Café Music Bar ££ ❷ Tastefully done out, this relaxed and unassuming bistro-style eatery – think exposed brick and low lighting – has an international menu and live music. The non-smoking section is a rare treat. The same can be said of the friendly service, which rises far above Kiev norms. ⓐ Kontraktova pl. 4 ⓣ 425 2474 ⓦ www.piano-cafe.com.ua ◷ 10.00–23.00 ⓝ Metro: Kontraktova Ploscha

Svitlytsia ££ ❸ Despite the Ukrainian name, this eatery serves French-style crêpes filled with anything from honey to caviar. ⓐ Andriivsky uzviz 13B ⓣ 425 3186 ◷ 11.00–23.00 ⓝ Metro: Kontraktova Ploscha

Podil's decimated Jewish population left such treasures as this synagogue

AFTER DARK

RESTAURANTS

Tsymes ££ ❹ Jewish cuisine (non-kosher) is the thing at this cellar eatery. The weekday set lunch offers especially persuasive value. The décor, which features attractive frescoes, is another draw for intimate Tsymes. ⓐ Sahaydachnoho 10/5 ⓣ 428 7579 ◔ 11.00–23.00

Marrakesh ££–£££ ❺ As its name implies, this restaurant has an Arabian theme. The menu is mainly couscous dishes, although not as spicy as one would find in the real Marrakech. ⓐ Sahaydachnoho 24 ⓣ 494 0494 ◔ 11.00–01.00 Ⓜ Metro: Kontraktova Ploscha

Mimino ££–£££ ❻ Considered one of the best restaurants in the city, its theme is based on a Soviet cult movie of the same name. The cuisine is Georgian, and features mainly lamb dishes, many of which are very spicy. A vegetarian menu is also available. ⓐ Spaska 10A ⓣ 417 3545 ⓦ www.karta.ua ◔ 11.00–01.00 Ⓜ Metro: Kontraktova Ploscha

Tequila House £££ ❼ Mexican cuisine served with any one of 20 types of tequila. ⓐ Spaska 8A ⓣ 417 0358 ⓦ www.karta.ua ◔ 12.00–23.00 Ⓜ Metro: Kontraktova Ploscha

BARS & CLUBS

Disco Radio Hall A small ship converted to a nightclub, which claims to have the longest bar in Europe. It features fashion shows on a transparent catwalk and pop music. Admission is free, but drinks are expensive. ⓐ Berth 6, Naberezhno-Khreschatytska ◔ 20.00–06.00 Ⓜ Metro: Kontraktova Ploscha

Plenty of ambience after dark in the streets of Kiev

Outer Kiev

Outside the compact central areas of the city, Kiev sprawls in all directions. Nondescript blocks of flats are ubiquitous and attractions for the casual visitor – apart from those listed here – are few and far between. The Tourist Hotel complex on the left bank of the Dnipro (see page 45) has good restaurants, bars and nightclubs. See the main city map (pages 62–3) for sights in greater Kiev and the 'Around Kiev' map (pages 118–19) for places further afield. With the exception of

JEWISH KIEV

Jews have played an important part in the history and culture of Kiev. From the 12th to 19th centuries, Jews played prominent roles in the political, cultural, business and scientific communities of the city. Sadly, as in many other parts of the world, the Jews became scapegoats in times of war and unrest: Cossacks, Tsars, Communists and Nazis all persecuted them. Before World War II, Jews made up 20 per cent of Kiev's population. Today it is only 3 per cent. Since independence, the Central Synagogue, in the city centre, and the Podil Synagogue have been returned to their rightful owners and rebuilt as places for Jews to worship. Golda Meir, former Prime Minister of Israel, was born in Kiev at Baseina 5A, before she emigrated to the United States with her family. There is a bust and a plaque dedicated to her at this address. Sholom Aleichem, a famous storyteller and author, was born just outside Kiev (see page 112), and there is a monument to him at Rognidynska 3. His writings inspired *Fiddler on the Roof*.

Bila Tserka, Chernobyl and Pereyaslav-Khmelnytsky, all the places of interest in this chapter can easily be reached by public transport.

SIGHTS & ATTRACTIONS

Babi Yar

This sobering site is dedicated to the memory of the tens of thousands of citizens, mainly Jewish, who were massacred here by the Nazis in World War II. From 29 to 31 September 1941, some 34,000 Jews were killed at Babi Yar, as were many more 'enemies of the Third Reich' during the rest of the Nazi occupation; in all, over 100,000 victims are believed to be buried here. During the 1970s, the Soviets erected a monument to the citizens who perished and, since independence in 1991, the construction of memorials has begun. The Children's

The moving memorial at Babi Yar

Memorial, dedicated to the murdered young, and the Menorah Monument, placed on the actual execution site, are a grim and chilling testament to the massacre. 24 hrs Metro: Dorohozhychi

Bila Tserkva

The largest city in the Kiev region after the capital, about an hour south of the centre of Kiev, Bila Tserkva is known for its many small, white churches and beautiful parks, including Oleksandriya park. It gained its place in Ukrainian history thanks to Bohdan Khmelnytsky, who signed a treaty with Poland here in 1651, making big concessions to the Poles. Within a year, Khmelnytsky broke the treaty, and drove the Poles out. The easiest way to visit is to take an organised tour; ask at the tourist office (see page 152) for details.

Chornobyl (Chernobyl)

This is the site of the world's worst nuclear disaster, 128 km (80 miles) from Kiev. There is not a lot to see there, so it is more of a 'been there,

NUCLEAR DISASTER

Early in the morning of 26 April 1986, the Number 4 reactor at the Chernobyl nuclear power plant literally blew its top and catapulted tonnes of radioactive material into the sky. Nearly 100 times the amount of radioactive material produced by the Hiroshima bomb blew west and north, leaving devastation in its path, and contaminating over 35,000 sq km (13,500 sq miles) of forest and farmland. Six days later, the wind would turn south and carry the radioactive cloud over an unsuspecting Kiev during the May Day celebrations.

Ironically, this nuclear explosion was the result of a safety test. The reactor was being powered down for maintenance on 26 April when the operators decided to test the emergency shutdown system. Due to operational errors, as well as a design flaw, the reactor overheated, resulting in a steam explosion, followed by the nuclear explosion.

The Soviets tried to cover up the accident, but, when the radioactive cloud reached Sweden, scientists there alerted the world. After the accident, the reactor and other radioactive material were covered in a large steel and concrete 'sarcophagus'. This cap is now disintegrating, but a new one is being prepared with international assistance.

Only two people died in the initial accident, but sadly 29 firemen were immediately sent in to clean up the mess. They were not given proper information or safety gear, and all died within weeks due to radiation poisoning. Since then, an estimated 5,000 more people have died as a result of the accident, and up to a million more may be affected in the long term by cancer, birth defects, heart disease and suicide. The aftermath of this disaster will continue to haunt Ukraine and Kiev for many years to come.

done that' type of destination for the curious. The radiation levels are now quite low, so visitors do not have to fear for their health. Desolate and overgrown landscapes and eerie, empty villages are the most notable sights, along with the massive concrete cap poured over the remains of the reactor. Visiting Chernobyl as an individual is not easy, as there is no regular transport, and there is a lot of red tape to clear in order to visit the site. Under-18s are prohibited. Taking a guided package tour is preferable, and takes all the hassle out of the visit. Costs for an individual tour are high, but decrease as the number in the group increases, with a group of ten or more getting the best deal. Some tour companies who go to Chernobyl are:

New Logic ⓐ Kreschatyk 42, 4th floor ⓣ 206 2200 ⓦ www.newlogic.ua ◷ 09.00–21.00 Mon–Fri, 10.00–21.00 Sat & Sun Ⓜ Metro: Teatralna

Panorama-Tour ⓐ Shota Rustaveli 8, office 3 ⓣ 502 6509 ⓦ http://panorama-tours.eu ◷ 09.00–19.00 Mon–Fri, 09.00–15.00 Sat Ⓜ Metro: Palats Sportu

Pereyaslav Khmelnytsky

This city is about 90 minutes south of Kiev, on the left bank of the River Dnipro. It was important in Kyivan Rus times (9th–13th centuries), but fell out of favour after Bohdan Khmelnytsky signed Ukraine over to the Tsars in 1654. Jewish writer Sholom Aleichem was born here, and there is a museum dedicated to him in the city. This is a good place to learn about Kyivan Rus, Cossacks and everyday life in rural Ukraine. There is a popular **Museum of Folk Architecture & Lifestyle** (ⓐ Litopysna 2 ◷ 10.00–17.00) and the beautiful Church of St Michael.

Pokrovska Convent

This convent was founded by the sister-in-law of Tsar Alexander II when she recovered from an illness after visiting the Caves Monastery. The Pokrovska Church, which looks like a cake decorated in pink, was built in 1889. St Mykola's (St Nikolai's) Cathedral, in white, blue and gold, was built in 1911. Both are designed in pure Tsarist Russian style. The convent is fairly close to the centre, but far enough out to have avoided any desecration during the turmoil of

St Mykola's Cathedral is one of the jewels of the Pokrovska Convent

the 20th century. Ⓐ Bekhteryevsky prov. 15 Ⓣ 486 7168 Ⓛ Services: 07.00 & 17.00 Ⓝ Metro: Lukyanivska

Pyrohovo Open-air Museum of Folk Architecture & Life

Located about 12 km (7 miles) south of Kiev in the town of Pyrohovo, this large open-air museum is made up of over 300 buildings dating back to the 16th century. These authentic buildings have been collected from all over Ukraine to form a 'village' depicting life in former times. Different areas of the museum cover different areas of Ukraine. Here you will see barns, schools, homes, churches, windmills and other buildings. Inside are exhibits such as stoves, clothing, ceramics, household utensils and farm equipment. In summer, actors dressed as peasants roam around and answer questions. They engage in traditional peasant activities, such as wood-carving, pottery, beekeeping and embroidery. On Sundays a traditional church service is held in one of the churches on site. Traditional Ukrainian meals are served at several locations. You'll get more out of it if you take a guided tour with one of the English-speaking guides. Ⓐ Chervonopraporna, Pyrohovo Ⓣ 526 5542 Ⓛ Museum: 10.00–17.00; grounds: sunrise–sunset Ⓝ Metro: Lybidska, then trolleybus 11 or *marshrutka* 172; Metro: Lukyanivska, then *marshrutka* 496 ⓘ Admission charge

RETAIL THERAPY

Darynok market

This well-established indoor market east of the city centre is one of Kiev's best. Dig through piles of goods brought in from China and Turkey, and be prepared to bargain. Ⓛ 09.00–20.00 Ⓝ Metro: Lisova

➊ *The beaches at Odessa are a gift to sun-worshippers*

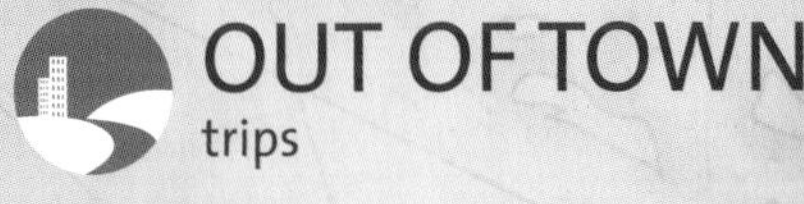

OUT OF TOWN
trips

Lviv (Lvov)

Lviv, also spelt 'Lvov' on English-language maps, is emerging as Ukraine's main tourist jewel. It has the untouched quality that Prague used to have, although, as the city is hosting several group matches during Euro 2012, this may change. The city is an architectural time capsule, with buildings representing periods from the 13th to 21st centuries. The heart of the city is the elegant Market Square, developed during the 16th to 18th centuries, and each of the 44 houses around it has its own story. No wonder UNESCO has recognised this area as a World Heritage site.

GETTING THERE

By air

Ukraine International Airlines (Ⓦ www.flyuia.com) offers regular flights between Kiev and Lviv for around 800–1,600hr. return; flight time is 70–80 minutes.

By rail or road

The cheapest options are the bus or the train, with several daily departures. The bus shouldn't cost much more than 100hr. one way, and takes nine to eleven hours. The overnight train takes eight to nine hours and costs 150hr. (standard) to 500hr. (luxury compartment).

SIGHTS & ATTRACTIONS

Apteka (Pharmacy) Museum

No antiseptic dispensary, this; in fact, it's one of the loveliest places in Lviv, and it's been knocking out prescriptions since 1735. The museum

The Dormition Church rises above the rooftops of Lviv

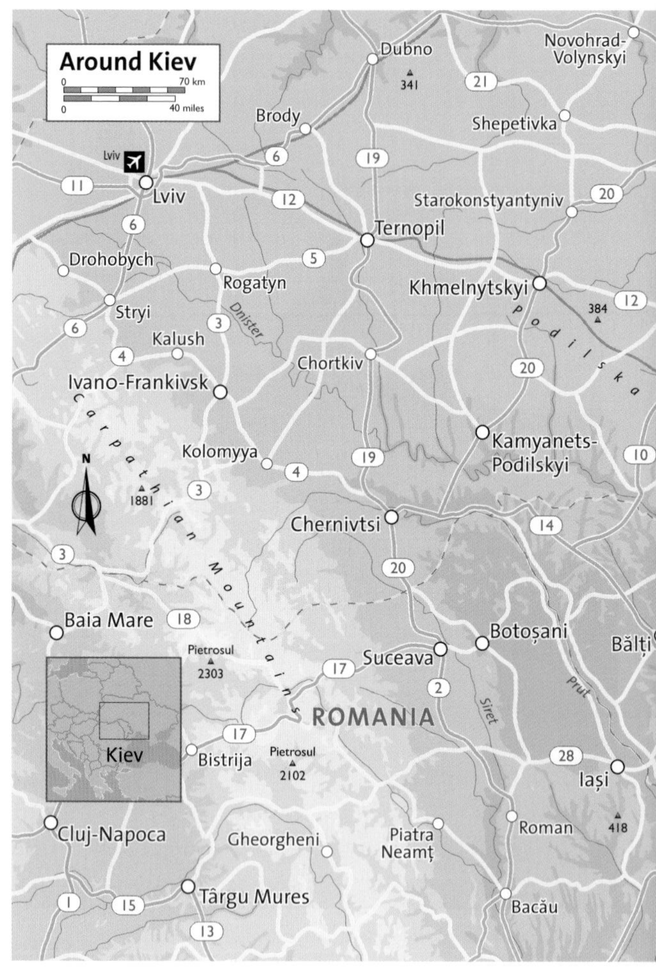
Around Kiev
0
70 km
0
40 miles
Lviv
Lviv
Dubno
341
Novohrad-Volynskyi
Brody
Shepetivka
Starokonstyantyniv
Ternopil
Drohobych
Rogatyn
Khmelnytskyi
Stryi
Dnister
384
Podilska
Kalush
Ivano-Frankivsk
Chortkiv
Carpathian Mountains
Kolomyya
Kamyanets-Podilskyi
N
1881
Chernivtsi
Baia Mare
Botoșani
Bălți
Pietrosul
2303
Suceava
Prut
Siret
ROMANIA
Kiev
Bistrija
Pietrosul
2102
Iași
418
Cluj-Napoca
Gheorgheni
Piatra Neamț
Roman
Târgu Mures
Bacău
11
6
12
19
21
20
5
3
4
10
14
18
17
2
28
1
15
13

KIEV
Chornobyl
Kiev Zulhany
Boryspil
Pyrohovo
Kiev Boryspil
Zhytomyr
Pereyaslav Khmelnytsky
Lubny
Berdychiv
Fastiv
Bila Tserkva
Skvyra
Sula
Tarashcha
Cherkasy
Kremenchuksk Vdskh
Smila
Vinnytsya
Zhashkiv
UKRAINE
Sinyukha
Novomirgorod
Tulchyn
270
Uman
Kirovohrad
Novoukrayinka
269
Balta
Pervomaysk
Buh
Rîbnita
Ananyiv
Voznesensk
Dubăsari Vdkhr
Tyligul
MOLDOVA
Berezivka
Snihurivka
Chişinău
CHIŞINĂU
Tiraspol
Mykolayiv
Tighina
Kherson
Dnipro
Cimişlia
Odessa International
Odessa
Black Sea
City
Large Town
Small Town
POI
Main Road
Minor Road
Airport
Railway
International border

rooms have a fascinating display of chemistry-set glasses, jars, tubes and documents that recount a sometimes bizarre history of diagnoses and speculative cures. ⓐ Drukarska 2 ⓣ (32) 235 7041 ◷ 09.00–18.00 Mon–Fri, 10.00–17.00 Sat & Sun ⓘ Admission charge

Bandinelli Palace Museum

This is the one-time palace of Signor Bandinelli, who, in 1629, initiated a communications revolution of his own by starting the city's – and some say Eastern Europe's – very first postal service. The museum has a long and varied career, having formerly been both the Museum of the History of the Postal Service and the Museum of Glass; today it forms part of the Historical Museum and, whether you're into stamps, glass or history, it is worth a visit for the beauty in which it has been left by painstaking restoration. ⓐ Rynok pl. 2 ⓣ (32) 272 0671 ◷ 10.00–17.30 Thur–Tues ⓘ Admission charge

Dzyga Gallery

This is an exhibition of contemporary and classic art, a concert hall with excellent acoustics, and a gallery shop where you can buy pieces of modern art and antiques. It also has a café, 'Under Clepsydra'. It is based inside the former Dominican monastery, with a cosy inner courtyard, and hosts a theatre studio, a cinema club and workshops for children. ⓐ Virmenska 35 ⓣ (32) 276 7420 ⓦ www.dzyga.com.ua ◷ 10.00–24.00

Lviv National Art Gallery

Sixty thousand exhibits back up this museum's claim of housing Ukraine's most extensive art collection; and yet its beginnings over a century ago carry the whiff of shame, for the initial collection, that of sugar king Ivan Yakovych, was actually contraband. Happily, it went legit and is now Lviv's National Art Gallery. ⓐ Stefanyka 3 ⓣ (32) 261 4647 ⓛ 11.00–18.00 Tues–Sat (10.00–17.00 in winter), 12.00–17.00 Sun. Last entry one hour before closing

Lviv Opera House

So atmospheric is the Opera House that, pause for a while and, if you're prone to auditory hallucinations, you may think you can hear Caruso's top C reverberating around the auditorium. While this establishment is still an ongoing operatic concern, its looks are what have made it famous – its silhouette graces Ukraine's bank notes. ⓐ Svobody prosp. 28 ⓣ (32) 272 8860 ⓦ www.lvivopera.org

Royal Mansion (Kornyact Palace) & Historical Museum

The Royal Mansion is the jewel in the Historical Museum's crown, thanks largely to its beautiful fixtures and fittings, many of which were gathered by Jan Sisisky. If you're particularly into heroic portraiture, this is a great place to visit to see how the superstars of old used to market their noble deeds. ⓐ Rynok pl. 6 ⓣ (32) 272 0671 ⓦ www.lhm.lviv.ua ⓛ 10.00–18.00 Thur–Tues (10.00–17.00 in winter) ⓘ Admission charge

Rynok Ploscha (Market Square)

Rynok is the epicentre of Lviv's architectural heritage. Here's why: the 19th-century town hall, with its neo-Renaissance tower; the Bandinelli Palace (also called the Black Mansion), with its striking façade, that was built for an Italian merchant; House No. 6, the Kornyakt House (also known as the Royal Mansion), with its row of sculpted knights along the rooftop; the Boyim Chapel, the burial chapel of a Hungarian merchant; and the Roman Catholic Cathedral, visited by Pope John Paul II in 2001.

RETAIL THERAPY

Folk Art Market There comes a point in every trip when the matter of souvenir and gift buying has to be confronted. There is no finer place to do so than here. This trove of (mainly) authentic handicraft and folk products is just the place to bag that essential Cossack shirt. ⓐ Vicheva pl. ⓛ 09.00–17.00

Letter Bookshop Book-lovers should head for the orange house off the southwestern corner of Rynok; there they will find one of the best bookshops in town. There is a good range of titles in English, including guidebooks to the city, as well as glossy coffee-table souvenirs to pore over once you get back home. The delicious snacks and very decent coffee in the cosy little café alongside may keep you longer than you expected. ⓐ Shevska 6 ⓣ (32) 294 8208 ⓛ 10.00–21.00 Mon–Sat, 11.00–21.00 Sun

Magnus Shopping Centre This five-storey modern shopping centre has just about everything you might want or need, including a restaurant with a free Wi-Fi hotspot on the fifth floor. ⓐ Shpytalna 1 ⓣ (32) 244 4265 ⓦ www.magnus-store.com ⓛ Shops: 10.00–21.00; restaurant: 09.00–23.00

SERVICES

Central Post Office The place for stamps, mobile-phone rentals and phone cards. ⓐ Slovatskoho 1 ⓣ (32) 261 5321 ⓛ 08.30–17.30 Mon–Sat

Internet Club Long-standing café offering 24-hour Internet access and other digital services. ⓐ D Dudayeva 12 ⓣ (32) 272 2738 ⓛ 24 hrs

Raiffeisen Bank Aval An easy-to-find, multi-service bank adjacent to the main post office. ⓐ Slovatskoho 1 ⓣ 0800 500 500 ⓦ www.aval.ua ⓗ 09.00–18.00 Mon–Fri

TAKING A BREAK

Celentano ££ This congenial pizzeria is extremely popular with the locals, and you can see why. What's more, it's one of those places where the freestyle mix-and-match toppings policy empowers you to create that pizza you've fantasised about for years. ⓐ Svobody prosp. 24 ⓣ (32) 237 0707 ⓦ www.pizza-celentano.com ⓗ 10.00–23.00

Livy Bereh ££ On the river's left bank, from where it takes its name, this arty eatery serves coffee and snacks, as well as more substantial comestibles. It is found beneath the Lviv Opera House, and the décor is made up of musical instruments. You can also draw a picture to commemorate your visit. ⓐ Svobody prosp. 28 ⓣ 050 430 0752 ⓗ 11.00–02.00

Svit Kavy £££ Lviv has a reputation for being a centre of excellence when it comes to coffee, and Svit Kavy is very much the place to go. ⓐ Katedralna pl. 6 ⓣ (32) 297 5675 ⓗ 08.00–22.00 Mon–Fri, 09.00–23.00 Sat & Sun

Tsukernia £££ This place is a cosy old-world café that serves up possibly the best desserts in all of Lviv. Dishes are based on old Galician recipes, and only natural ingredients are used. ⓐ Staroyevreyska 3 ⓣ (32) 235 6949 ⓦ www.cukiernia.com.ua ⓗ 10.00–22.00

Viennese Café £££ This is the venue to set your mouth a-drool if you're partial to a classic Austro-Hungarian nosh up. If your mind's not absolutely set on something else, it would seem a shame not to try the sauerkraut. The café is just by the old Jesuit Church and, on sunny days, chairs fan out across the terrace onto Pidkovy ploscha. ⓐ Svobody prosp. 12 ⓣ (32) 272 2021 ⓛ 09.00–23.30

AFTER DARK

RESTAURANTS

Vezha Kramariv ££ Set in a restored medieval tower on the fringe of Lviv's Old Town, this restaurant will have you feeling like a conquering invader as you tuck into a range of Ukrainian and European dishes. You must climb the tall stairs to get to its dining halls, but when you get there, you can relax near an open fire. A good place to take in the flavour of old Lviv. ⓐ Svobody prosp. 16–18 ⓣ (32) 272 3939 ⓛ 24 hrs

Grand Hotel Restaurant £££ When you hunger for a little old-world flair, head for the Grand Restaurant. It has Italian and Ukrainian cuisine, and is definitely the place for a sophisticated palate, as well as business lunches and romantic dinners. Its summer terrace offers a nice view over the main street of Lviv. ⓐ Svobody prosp. 13 ⓣ (32) 272 4091 ⓦ www.grandhotel.lviv.ua ⓛ 12.00–24.00

BARS & CLUBS

Art-Cafe 'Flat 35' If it's sitting outside watching the world go by that grabs you, come here; if you're taken by the fact that this is a magnet for arty types who want to relax in an arty way, ditto. ⓐ Virmenska 35 ⓣ (32) 297 5612 ⓦ www.dzyga.com.ua ⓛ 10.00–23.00

Robert Doms Beer House Oozing quirky history, this subterranean drinking den occupies what was once a beer vault for the adjacent brewery. Litre-sized receptacles lend themselves to the hard-core drinker, and there is a similarly oversized television screen that

Vezha Kramariv has superb food and a fantastic setting

broadcasts sport. Live bands also feature. ⓐ Kleparivska 18 ⓣ (32) 242 2594 ⓦ www.robertdoms.lviv.ua ⓗ 12.00–24.00

Split This club and show-bar also boasts strippers – for that sophisticated evening out! ⓐ Mitskevycha pl. 7 ⓣ (32) 242 2200 ⓦ www.split.lviv.ua ⓗ 24 hrs

ACCOMMODATION

George £–££ First-class rooms have TV, hairdryers, Internet access and refrigerators. Second-class accommodation requires you to share a bathroom, though that could be a small price to pay to sleep where Balzac, Jean-Paul Sartre and Liszt have all spent a night. However, the unsympathetic renovation the hotel has recently undergone would probably not have been to the tastes of that creative trio. ⓐ Mitskevycha pl. 1 ⓣ (32) 232 6236 ⓦ www.georgehotel.com.ua

Dnister ££ This hotel is located in the historic heart of the city and is a handy 6 km (4 miles) from the airport and 3 km (2 miles) from the railway station. The atmosphere is delightfully dignified – very old-school European, with an abundance of modern amenities. ⓐ Matejka 6 ⓣ (32) 297 4317 ⓦ www.dnister.lviv.ua

Hetman ££ This reasonably priced hotel has rooms equipped with TV and radio. The drawback is its location, outside the touristy Old Town area. Still, if pennies are tight, this is a sensible solution. ⓐ Volodomyra Velykoho 50 ⓣ (32) 230 1391 ⓦ www.hetman.lviv.ua

Nton ££ Opened in 2001 and situated about 3 km (2 miles) from the centre of town, this hotel is quite a success story and has become a bit of a haunt for Ukrainian and Russian film stars staying in Lviv. It has grown to over 60 rooms and suites, decorated in a simple and modern style. Room prices include breakfast. ⓐ Shevchenka 154B ⓣ (32) 233 3123 ⓦ www.hotelnton.lviv.ua

Zamok Leva ££ This moderately priced, clean and pleasant hotel was built as a mock-castle in 1898 by an Austrian architect. The hotel is located in the elite housing area of Lviv. There are some very famous names scribbled in its register, including Mikhail Gorbachev and Victor Yushchenko. Services include free Wi-Fi, television and fax. ⓐ Hlinky 7 ⓣ (32) 297 1563 ⓦ www.lioncastlehotel.com

Eney ££–£££ This is a small, very modern hotel, and with only 15 rooms available it would be wise to book well in advance. Amenities include TV, minibar and Wi-Fi services. Breakfast is included in the price, and children under the age of 6 stay for free in their parents' room. ⓐ Shimzeriv 2 ⓣ (32) 276 8799 ⓦ www.eney.lviv.ua

Volter ££–£££ Sister hotel of the Nton (see opposite), the Volter opened in 2004. The smart, simply decorated rooms are all equipped with TV, internet and telephone. It's located about 3 km (2 miles) from the city centre. ⓐ Lypynskoho 60A ⓣ (32) 294 8888 ⓦ www.hotelvolter.com.ua

Grand Hotel £££ This is the poshest place to stay in Lviv, perfectly situated close to the Opera House. Basking in its 1898 belle-époque grandeur, the hotel features well-appointed rooms, a health club with a beautiful indoor swimming pool, fine restaurants and helpful staff who speak English. ⓐ Svobody prosp. 13 ⓣ (32) 272 4042 ⓦ www.grandhotel.lviv.ua

Odessa

Odessa deserves its title of 'Pearl of the Black Sea'. Catherine the Great once imagined that it might become the 'St Petersburg of the South' and encouraged immigrants to settle here. Its history and its role as a trading port have enabled Odessa to grow into a cosmopolitan city, more Mediterranean in outlook than Eastern European. The locals are cultured, stylish and savvy, and its lively nightlife and agreeable climate have made it a favourite resort for decades. Although part of the city has definitely seen better days, it retains a lively atmosphere.

Odessa will fill you with a sense of déjà vu, particularly if you have seen Sergei Eisenstein's classic film *The Battleship Potemkin*, which makes use of the Potemkin Steps leading to the harbour from Primorsky bulvar. Russian, rather than Ukrainian, is its first language.

GETTING THERE

By air

One of the several daily internal flights between Kiev and Odessa will cost about 800hr. return, and the flight time is around 90 minutes.

By rail

Trains travel daily from Kiev to Odessa, costing about 500hr. for a luxury compartment or 120hr. for standard class.

By road

The seven-hour trip from Kiev to Odessa costs between 125hr. and 175hr., depending on the type of bus.

The historic Potemkin Steps

A VARIETY OF BEACHES

The architecture and general ambience, rather than specific sights, are the attractions of Odessa. People head to the beaches to see and be seen. The atmosphere is reminiscent of the Victorian English seaside, with its sideshows, cafés and bars. Closest to the city centre are Arkadia and Lanzheron beaches. Arkadia is the liveliest for hanging out, while Lanzheron has a more family-oriented atmosphere. Both beaches are crowded and dirty, and swimming is not recommended. The further south you travel, the less busy, and cleaner, the beaches become. Delphin and Fontan beaches are both clean and safe, even for children.

For a few years now, a major clean-up effort has been taking place, and the local government has declared that all the beaches are safe for swimming. However, you should use your own judgement and, if in doubt, don't dive in.

CULTURE

Archaeology Museum

This 200-year-old building makes a lovely environment in which to study the glory that was Greece, the wonder that was Rome and the absolute splendour that was Egypt. Nearly 2,000 exhibits justify the superlatives that are heaped on the ancients' ability to fashion beauty, and there are some fine antique statues in the vestibule. ⓐ Lanzheronovskaya 4 ⓣ (48) 722 0171 ⓦ www.archaeology.odessa.ua ◷ 10.00–17.00 Tues–Sun ❶ Admission charge

Fine Arts Museum

This is one of those priceless museums whose collection you're simply not going to find anywhere else. Both Ukrainian and European art are on display here, and it's the former that really sets the heart a-flutter; there's an astonishing set of Russian icons and paintings by Serov and Kandinsky among many other works by artists who, although less well known, on the evidence displayed here were no less gifted. ⓐ Sofievskaya 5A ⓣ (48) 723 8272 ⓒ 11.00–18.00 Wed–Mon ⓘ Admission charge

Historic Defence of Odessa Museum

This museum is dedicated to the defenders of Odessa in World War II. Although the city fell to the Germans and Romanians in October 1941 after a heroic defence, the partisans continued to harass the occupiers until it was freed in April 1944. The best part of the museum is outside the building itself – a large area packed with tanks, anti-aircraft guns and even a submarine. Inside the four-room museum are posters, pictures and small arms dating from World War II. ⓐ Dacha Kovalevskogo 150 ⓣ (48) 244 4527 ⓒ 10.00–17.30 Sat–Thur

History & Local Lore Museum

This museum's collection amounts to a comprehensive visual encyclopedia of the art produced in – and inspired by – Odessa since medieval times. The 'Sister Cities' display avoids self-obsession as it focuses on the many cities with which Odessa is twinned or has close ties. The architecture, politics and culture of bygone times are also explored in the extensive galleries. ⓐ Gavannaya 4 ⓣ (48) 272 8490 ⓒ 10.00–17.00 Sat–Thur ⓘ Admission charge

Musical & Comedy Theatre

The modern building is lovely, but save your money for performances of the Philharmonic Orchestra. ⓐ Panteleymonovskaya 3 ⓣ (48) 725 0924 ⓦ www.operetta.od.ua

Odessa Museum of Western & Eastern Art

The collection in this museum, which is set out in three sections (Ancient, Western European and Eastern Arts), shows how inspiring their meeting can be. The interior of the building could do with a little renovation, but the exhibitions contain works by Strozzi and Maniasco, as well as wonderful collections from Iran, Tibet, China, India and Japan. ⓐ Pushkinskaya 9 ⓣ (48) 722 4815 ⓦ www.oweamuseum.odessa.ua ⓛ 10.00–17.00 Thur–Tues

Opera House

Is there a prettier building – inside and out – in Odessa? Back with a bang after reconstruction, the Opera House is now firing on all cylinders, offering night after night of some of the finest operatic and balletic performances in Europe today. ⓐ Tchaikovskogo 1 ⓣ (48) 780 1509 ⓦ www.opera-ballet.tm.odessa.ua

Philharmonic Theatre

This is the home of the Odessa Philharmonic, the best regional orchestra of the former Soviet Union. Unfortunately the orchestra does not perform during the summer months. ⓐ Bunina 15 ⓣ (48) 725 6903 ⓦ www.odessaphilharmonic.org

Port Museum

This museum illustrates the history of the port of Odessa through photographs, maps and documents, and is now Odessa's main

Odessa's Opera House

museum of all things nautical, since the venerable Fleet Museum of Odessa and its contents were lost in a fire. One of its halls contains a 5-m (16-ft) model of the port. Lanzheronovsky Spusk 2 (48) 729 3857 10.00–17.00 Mon–Fri

RETAIL THERAPY

7th Kilometre This market, whose prosaic name signifies the fact that it lies 7 km (4 miles) from the centre of the city, is the largest in Ukraine. Off Ovidiopol highway 24 hrs Bus: 2–7 & 16

Deribasovskaya A little more traditional, this is Odessa's main commercial street, filled with all kinds of souvenir stores. Matryoshka dolls, hand-painted wooden boxes, embroidery and Soviet-era pins and medals all make good souvenirs.

Tolkuchka This is Odessa's weekend flea market, a huge bazaar filled with all kinds of goodies. The central part is on Privozna Street at the southeastern end of Aleksandrovsky prospekt, within walking distance of the Central Railway Station. Ⓛ 09.00–15.00 Sat & Sun

TAKING A BREAK

RESTAURANTS

Estrellita ££ A very short distance from the Potemkin Steps, this is one of the best Tex-Mex restaurants in Ukraine. It has two floors, a bar in the basement and a restaurant. There is also live music in the evening at weekends. ⓐ Ekaterininskaya 1 ⓣ (48) 237 2920 Ⓛ 24 hours

Kumanets ££ Word gets around about joints that serve first-rate Ukrainian food against a background of great service. So reserve. ⓐ Gavannaya 7 ⓣ (48) 237 6946 Ⓛ 11.00–24.00

Zara Pizzara ££ A good spot for a breakfast, lunch or dinner. It is one of the few places in Odessa with a salad bar. The pizza is great too, and the lower floor is non-smoking. ⓐ Rishelyevskaya 5 ⓣ (48) 728 8888 Ⓛ 07.15–23.00 Mon–Fri, 07.15–01.00 Sat

Khutorok £££ This 19th-century seaside restaurant offers fabulous European and Ukrainian cuisine, three banquet halls, a summer terrace and live music. ⓐ Shevchenko Park, just up from Lanzheron beach ⓣ (48) 735 3873 ⓦ www.khutorok.od.ua Ⓛ 12.00–24.00

Mick O'Neil's Irish Pub £££ This little taste of Dublin in Ukraine boasts 150 dishes. But the secret draw of its siren song is real-deal Guinness. ⓐ Deribasovskaya 13 ⓣ (48) 721 5333 Ⓛ 24 hrs

AFTER DARK

CLUBS & SHOWS

Captain Morgan This legendary nightclub covers two floors, holds 500 people and yet only has 150 seats, so don't go in the hope of having a nice sit down as you enjoy DJs, VJs and PJs from Kiev, Moscow and Western Europe. ⓐ Zhukovskogo 30 ⓣ (48) 728 8482 ⓦ www.morgan-club.com.ua ⓑ 10.00–08.00

Ibiza DJs and go-go dancers make this one of Odessa's more 'swinging' spots. It is a little retro, but it's undeniably lively. ⓐ Arkadia beach ⓣ (48) 777 0205 ⓦ www.ibiza.ua ⓑ 21.00–late Thur–Sun

Itaka This seaside amphitheatre hosts concerts by Russian pop artists, as well as practitioners of many other intriguing genres. ⓐ Arkadia beach ⓣ (48) 234 9188 ⓑ Restaurant: 09.00–late May–Sept; disco: 21.00–late May–Sept; event times vary

ACCOMMODATION

Hotels in Odessa grade themselves, so a three-star hotel in the city may not bear any comparison with a three-star hotel anywhere else in the world. The grading system tends to be based on physical space rather than amenities, and bad service or worn and neglected interiors don't count. If your wallet is really empty, the cheapest accommodation to be found is a room in someone's home. To find one, go to the station and look for a person, usually an older woman, with a sign reading 'KOMHATA' (*komnata* means 'room'). Be sure to ask if hot water is available. The going rate is about 50–100hr. a night.

Tsentralnyy £ This centrally located hotel has a fair bit of history, being one of the oldest in the city. It's worth poking your nose in to admire the other-worldly interior. ⓐ Preobrazhenskaya 40 ⓣ (48) 726 8406 ⓦ www.centralhotel.od.ua

Victoriya ££ This hotel is situated close to the sea and the famous Arkadia beach. It is moderately priced and provides everything you might reasonably need. ⓐ Genuezskaya 24A ⓣ (48) 746 5296 ⓦ http://victoriya.com.ua

Chernoye More ££–£££ Located in the centre of Odessa, this hotel is only a ten-minute walk from the railway station. It is also very close to one of the city beaches. Rooms are plain but nice, and are equipped with a bath or shower, TV, minibar and telephone. ⓐ Rishelyevskaya 59 ⓣ (48) 230 0904 ⓦ www.bs-hotel.com.ua

Londonskaya £££ Sitting right in the middle of the city, Odessa's oldest luxury hotel has fantastic views of the Black Sea and the famous Potemkin Steps. Non-smoking rooms are available, and there is an excellent restaurant on-site. ⓐ Primorsky bul. 11 ⓣ (48) 738 0110 ⓦ www.londred.com

Stock up on currency as soon as you arrive

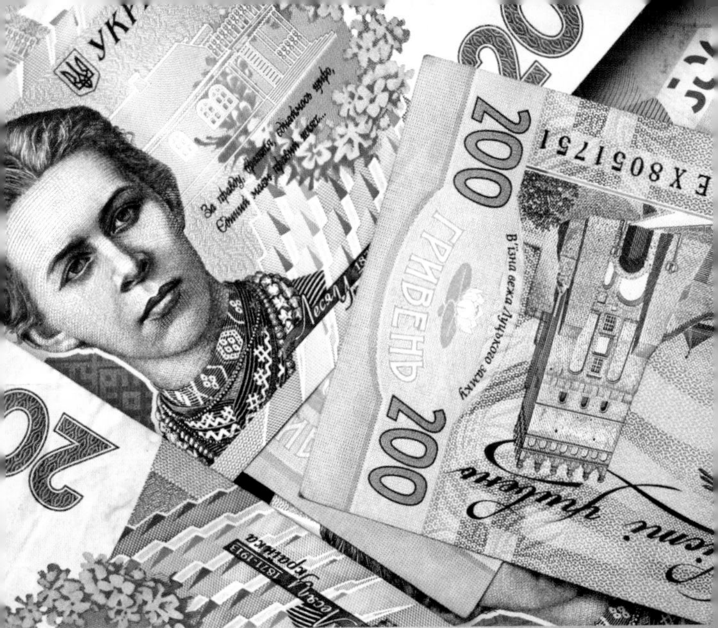

PRACTICAL
information

Directory

GETTING THERE

By air

Kiev is served by most major airlines, flying from most major European cities. British Airways, Air France, Austrian Airlines, KLM and Lufthansa have regular flights there. The two airlines of Ukraine – Ukraine International Airlines and Aerosvit – fly to most major European cities. Aerosvit also has twice-weekly flights to Toronto, and six flights a week to New York (JFK). Austrian Airlines has the most experience of flying into Ukraine, and many airlines have connections in Vienna. Contact numbers in Kiev are given below.

Aerosvit ⓣ 490 3490 ⓦ www.aerosvit.com
Air France ⓣ 496 3575 ⓦ www.airfrance.ua
Austrian Airlines ⓣ 492 7232 ⓦ www.aua.com
British Airways ⓣ 585 5050 ⓦ www.ba.com
KLM ⓣ 490 2490 ⓦ www.klm.com
Lufthansa ⓣ 490 3800 ⓦ www.lufthansa.com
Ukraine International Airlines ⓣ 581 5050 ⓦ www.flyuia.com

Many people are aware that air travel emits CO_2, which contributes to climate change. You may be interested in the possibility of lessening the environmental impact of your flight through the charity **Climate Care** (ⓦ www.jpmorganclimatecare.com), which offsets your CO_2 by funding environmental projects around the world.

By rail

The train service to Kiev from Western Europe is very good and connects through Berlin. A direct journey from the UK by rail will involve a cross-Channel ferry or the Eurostar to Brussels or Paris as the first leg of your journey.

The ultra-modern metro subway

The Berlin–Kiev section takes the best part of a day, sometimes a little longer, and costs upwards of 1,500hr. – see **Rail Europe** (ⓦ www.raileurope.co.uk). The monthly *Thomas Cook European Rail Timetable* has up-to-date schedules for train services to and within Ukraine.

Eurostar ⓣ (UK) 08705 186186 ⓦ www.eurostar.com

Thomas Cook European Rail Timetable ⓣ (UK) 01733 416477, (USA) 1 800 322 3834 ⓦ www.thomascookpublishing.com

Ukrainian official rail information ⓦ www.uz.gov.ua (in Ukrainian and Russian only).

For English-language train timetables for Russia and Ukraine, see ⓦ www.poezda.net or ⓦ www.bahn.de. Both sites provide reliable information on Ukrainian rail routes.

By road

Driving your own car into Ukraine is not recommended. To start with, few of the border guards speak English. On entry, you will have to sign papers promising to remove the car from the country within two months, which could prove difficult if your car is stolen or wrecked, which happens to a lot of cars with foreign licence plates. Car insurance is mandatory in Ukraine, as is an international driver's licence.

If you must drive to Kiev from Western Europe, it is easiest to follow Highway E-40, which runs from Brussels through Germany and Poland and into Ukraine, through Lviv and directly into Kiev. There are also good routes to Kiev from the former Eastern bloc countries that border Ukraine.

Speed limits are 60 kph (37 mph) in cities, 90 kph (56 mph) on secondary highways and 130 kph (81 mph) on main highways. There is zero tolerance for drinking and driving, and breathalysers were introduced in 2010. If you are stopped for a traffic violation, you can pay the fine at a bank office (or make a 'donation' on the spot).

ENTRY FORMALITIES

Visiting Ukraine as a tourist has been easier since visa requirements were greatly relaxed. Visitors from EU countries, Switzerland, Liechtenstein, Canada, the USA and Japan no longer require visas to enter Ukraine if they are staying for 90 days or less. Visitors from most other countries, and all those wanting to stay longer, still need a visa, which can be obtained from any Ukrainian embassy or consulate. Visas are also still required for students, and for people doing business in the country.

On entry

As of autumn 2010, immigration cards were abolished, so you should no longer be asked for one. You will not be required to fill out customs forms if you are bringing in less than the equivalent of US$10,000 in other currencies, and have no declarable goods. Otherwise, customs forms are available in English on flights into Ukraine, but are normally only in Ukrainian at border crossings for cars, trains and buses. You are allowed to bring in 1 litre (2 pints) of spirits or 2 litres (4 pints) of wine or 10 litres (17 pints) of beer, and 200 cigarettes. Prohibited items include illegal drugs, weapons, radioactive items, plants and animals. Certain types of propaganda, especially those promoting genocide, racial hatred and overthrow of the government, are also prohibited. You may be required to purchase medical insurance issued by the state when entering the country.

Customs

Customs and Immigration is still quite bureaucratic, with long queues, so expect to take up to an hour to clear. Be patient – you will get through. Most immigration officials at Boryspil Airport speak English, but few of them at other border crossings do.

Footbridge over the River Dnipro

Be sure to always keep your passport with you, as you may be asked to present it at any time by the police. Also retain any customs forms, as you will need to present these when leaving the country.

On exit

You can expect to have your passport checked and customs form reviewed before you leave Ukraine. There are restrictions on what you can take out of the country. It is forbidden to remove certain Ukrainian antiquities and icons. There are also restrictions on the amount of local currency, alcohol and caviar that you can take out. Most reputable merchants are aware of the restrictions, so ask them before you buy these items.

WHAT TO TAKE

Kiev is one of those destinations where you won't want to pack lightly. Items that we consider readily available and easy to obtain may not be, even in the capital city. Some things not to leave home without include good toilet paper, a multi-purpose knife (with a screwdriver head), hand sanitiser, torch (flashlight) and a sewing kit. A mini-first-aid kit is a good idea too, stocked with antiseptic cream, anti-diarrhoea pills, tummy settlers, nasal decongestant or cold remedies, painkillers and plasters. If you wear contact lenses, make sure you have an adequate supply of cleaning solution. For the most part you should be able to buy your cosmetic needs in Kiev, but if you have particular favourites, take a supply along.

A small Ukrainian or Russian dictionary will be of great help (to supplement the phrases given in this book). The *Thomas Cook Eastern European Phrasebook* has a wide range of useful phrases in Ukrainian (and Russian, useful in Odessa). Take plenty of business cards – Ukrainians are fond of these and take delight in the ritual exchange of them.

Don't be afraid to take your stylish clothing to Kiev. If ever there was a city that is a slave to fashion, Kiev is it. Residents always wear their best out in public and will expect you to do the same. People here dress for dinner, for a performance at a theatre and for social outings. If you are heading to Kiev in the winter, dress warmly from the inside out. In temperatures that can drop to -15°C (5°F), you will want some good thermal underwear, warm socks that rise as high as your knees, insulated waterproof boots, lined gloves and a warm hat that covers your ears – and a nice long scarf to wrap several times around your neck to keep out the cold wind. By contrast, in summer, when the temperature and the humidity make it steamy, you will also want to dress in layers that you can peel off and still maintain a level of modesty. If you plan on travelling by overnight train, say to Odessa, don't forget to pack a pair of pyjamas or a T-shirt and jogging bottoms.

Pack it all up in an unassuming bag. Although Ukrainians may dress well, and will pay particular attention to the quality of your footwear, luggage is not an area in which you will want to stand out. A smart, good-looking, high-quality case is an invitation to a robbery. If you have a choice, select a hard-sided case, as the soft-sided ones can be slashed open.

MONEY

The official currency of Ukraine is the hryvnia, abbreviated to hr. (or UAH in bureaux de change and banks). The hryvnia is divided into 100 kopecks. Coins come in denominations of 1, 5, 10, 25 and 50 kopecks and 1hr. Notes come in 1, 2, 5, 10, 20, 50, 100, 200 and 500hr. denominations. At the end of 2008, the Ukrainian hryvnia lost about

50 per cent of its value against the dollar and euro due to the economic slowdown. Few shops and restaurants will accept euros, pounds sterling or US dollars.

It will be necessary to buy some hryvnia upon arrival, as it is virtually impossible to obtain the currency outside the country. When you exchange money, make sure the notes you are changing are new and in good condition, as most moneychangers will not accept tattered or torn notes, or any that are not of the issuing country's latest design. Most hotels offer currency exchange and you will find bureau de change kiosks on major streets, so you should shop around a bit to get the best exchange rate.

ATMs, or Bankomats as they are locally known, are abundant, and the best way to manage your money in Kiev is to take it out in hryvnia from an ATM when you need it. Exchange rates are generally as good as or better than those at bureaux de change. Some banks and ATMs may restrict the amount of cash you can withdraw.

Major credit cards are readily accepted by most major hotels, many restaurants, and some shops. However, it is always wise to carry some cash in case you find a merchant who will not accept them. Traveller's cheques, however, are not normally accepted, and should be avoided. A few banks will take them, but normally only in US dollars; cashing them can be lengthy and difficult, and you will be charged at least 2 per cent commission.

HEALTH, SAFETY & CRIME

Good travel insurance covering medical problems, personal injury and loss of property is an absolute essential for all trips to Kiev.

Do not drink tap water. The water supply and sewerage systems in Kiev are in very bad shape, so do not brush your teeth with it either, and avoid ice cubes in drinks unless you know that they have

TRAVEL INSURANCE

However you book your city break, it is important to take out adequate personal travel insurance for the trip. For peace of mind the policy should give cover for medical expenses, loss, theft, repatriation, personal liability and cancellation expenses. If you are hiring a vehicle you should also check that you are appropriately insured and make sure that you take relevant insurance documents and your driving licence with you.

been made with clean or boiled water. Good mineral water is available everywhere, and at reasonable prices, so there is no reason to drink tap water. Despite precautions, many visitors do develop diarrhoea ('Gorbachev Gallop' in this part of the world), so bring along an anti-diarrhoea drug such as Imodium. If you do catch a bug, take the medicine, drink lots of fluids and wait it out. It should clear up in 24 hours; if it does not, it is time to get medical help.

Visitors should make sure that their relevant vaccinations are up to date, and those planning to go to a wooded area outside the city should be immunised against tick-borne encephalitis. Although pharmacies are abundant in Kiev and are well stocked with medicines and other supplies, you should bring your own prescription drugs (in their original container), and, if required, your own sterile syringes.

Smoking

Despite the 2006 regulations against smoking in Ukraine, you can still expect a lot of second-hand smoke in just about any restaurant or bar, although under law they must offer no-smoking sections.

Cigarettes for those that want them are sold everywhere, and are very inexpensive.

Radiation

No one can forget the Chernobyl disaster. Fortunately for today's visitors, most of the radioactive cloud blew north and west, away from Kiev, although some radioactivity did reach the city. Today, radiation levels have dropped to normal, and visitors have nothing to fear. Day trips to the Chernobyl site are one of the more popular 'tourist attractions', and the higher radiation levels at Chernobyl are not considered dangerous if you do not stay too long. Nevertheless, Chernobyl is off-limits to under-18s and may not be an advisable destination for pregnant women.

Crime

Although organised crime is still a problem in Ukraine, the perpetrators tend to leave tourists alone as long as they do not interfere in their business. Crime against visitors is about average for a large European city. It is virtually impossible for foreigners to 'blend into' the local scene, so you can easily be a target for pickpockets, muggers and bag snatchers.

Take the normal precautions against crime when in Kiev. Do not flash expensive jewellery or large amounts of cash around, or exhibit other signs of wealth. Try to use ATMs that are inside banks, and be mindful of people watching as you withdraw cash. Crowded areas, such as bus and railway stations and busy markets, should be avoided, as they are magnets for petty criminals. Do not carry bags of goods on to crowded metro trains, buses or trams, as you may find the bag slashed and the goods gone. If possible, do not travel alone, especially at night and if you have been drinking.

Cars should be locked and parked in open or well-lit areas, with any valuables, such as jewellery, cameras, mobile phones and computers, locked in the boot or otherwise kept out of sight.

OPENING HOURS

The official working week is 09.00–17.00 Monday to Friday, although some offices work 10.00–18.00. Many offices still close for lunch at 13.00–14.00. Some banks close early at 16.00, while others stay open until 20.00. Bigger shops stay open later, until 20.00 or 21.00, seven days a week. Restaurants tend to open at noon and stay open until 23.00. Cafés and cafeterias open earlier, at 08.00 or 09.00, and many close at 18.00 or 19.00. Museum hours are 09.00–17.00, although some stay open until 18.00. Most museums close two days a week, although the days vary, and some close during the last week of the month for cleaning.

TOILETS

Public toilets are generally nasty in Kiev. Many are of the old hole-in-the-floor type. Most also charge about 1hr. to use. The better ones are at the new Central Railway Station and in underground shopping centres. The worst are found in public parks and at beaches. The toilets in fast-food restaurants, such as McDonald's, are normally good, but can deteriorate as the day goes on.

CHILDREN

Bringing children, especially very young ones, to Kiev can be problematic. Dealing with the bureaucracy and worrying about drinking water and hygiene are made much worse with children in tow. Furthermore, you may find that some of the attractions in Kiev are of little interest to your children.

COMMUNICATIONS

Internet

Internet access is not a problem in Kiev, although some of the servers can be erratic. Almost all hotels have a business centre with Internet access and Wi-Fi hotspots. The Central Post Office has an excellent Internet café on the second floor, and there are many others scattered throughout the city, including:

Bunker Computer Club Artema 11A 272 4860 24 hrs
Trolleybus: 16, 18 to Lvivska Ploscha

Matritsa Internet Café Shota Rustaveli 8 235 9462 24 hrs
Metro: Palats Sportu

TELEPHONING UKRAINE

The country code for Ukraine is 380, and the city code for Kiev is 44. To call Kiev from your home country, dial the international access code (usually 00) followed by 380, followed by 44 and the local seven-digit number. City codes for Lviv and Odessa are 32 and 48 respectively.

TELEPHONING ABROAD

To make an international phone call from Kiev, dial 0, wait for a second dial tone, dial 0 again, then continue with the country code, area code (dropping the first 0 if there is one) and local number you require. The country code for Australia is 61, the UK 44, the Republic of Ireland 353, South Africa 27, New Zealand 64, USA and Canada 1. If you need assistance making an international call, an English-speaking operator can be reached by dialling 8192.

Phone

If calling Kiev from elsewhere in Ukraine, you will need to dial the city code (44) before the seven-digit numbers listed in this guide. If you are making a local call within Kiev, you can drop the code. The same goes for Lviv (32) and Odessa (48).

Public phones take either coins or phone cards, which are available at any post office. Most post offices also have international phone booths. You must pay an advance deposit in order to use the phone, with the balance being returned at the end of the call.

Most European mobile phones should work in Kiev – check with your provider – but calls can be very expensive. If you are planning to make a lot of calls, purchase a Ukrainian SIM card from any phone store or street vendor.

Post

Kiev's Central Post Office is located in the centre of the city on Maidan Nezalezhnosti. It is huge and usually busy. Besides regular postal services, there are an Internet café, fax services and international telephones. There are about 170 post offices in Kiev, so finding one should not be a problem – just ask for *poshta*. Postboxes are hung on buildings throughout the city; they are yellow with the dark blue Cyrillic letters ПОШТА.

Although outgoing post is slow, it is quite reliable. Incoming post is not reliable, and it is better to use email or couriers such as FedEx or DHL. Outgoing post should be sent airmail, and international postcards need to be placed inside an envelope. Letters to Europe take about ten days; letters to North America take two to three weeks. International letters cost about 6hr. to mail. International mail can be addressed in Latin characters.

Central Post Office ⓐ Khreschatyk 22 ⓣ 323 2020 ⓦ www.ukrposhta.

com 08.00–21.00 Mon–Sat, 09.00–19.00 Sun Metro: Maidan Nezalezhnosti

DHL Vasylkivska 2 490 2600 www.dhl.com.ua 08.00–20.00 Mon–Fri, 09.00–14.00 Sat

Federal Express Kikvidze 44 495 2020 09.00–18.00 Mon–Fri Metro: Vydubychi

MEDIA

English-language newspapers and magazines are available in Kiev. The *Kyiv Post* weekly (www.kyivpost.com) gives good, reliable information on everything from politics to entertainment.

What's On (www.whatson-kiev.com) provides up-to-the-minute information on restaurants, nightlife, entertainment and special events. Both of these publications, as well as imported English-language newspapers and magazines, are available at most major hotels, many news-stands, and at English-language bookshops.

ELECTRICITY

The standard is 220 V, 50 Hz. Most sockets use the standard continental European plug with two round pins; UK visitors will need an adaptor – North Americans a transformer as well – to use their appliances in Ukraine.

TRAVELLERS WITH DISABILITIES

Kiev is not user-friendly to those with mobility problems, although this is slowly changing. Steps are steep and curbs are high. The Central Railway Station does have lifts for wheelchairs, but the rest of the public transport system does not have anything to aid accessibility. Some hotels and restaurants, however, do have facilities for travellers with disabilities. For information in your own country, contact:

Access-able ⓦ www.access-able.com
Disabled Persons Assembly For New Zealand-based travellers. ⓐ 4/173–175 Victoria Street, Wellington, New Zealand ⓣ (04) 801 9100 ⓦ www.dpa.org.nz
Irish Wheelchair Association ⓐ Blackheath Drive, Clontarf, Dublin 3 ⓣ (01) 818 6400 ⓦ www.iwa.ie
National Disability Services For Australia-based travellers. ⓐ Locked Bag 3002, 33 Thesiger Court, Deakin West, ACT 2600 ⓣ (02) 6283 3200 ⓦ www.nds.org.au
RADAR UK-based advice. ⓣ 020 7250 3222 ⓦ www.radar.org.uk
Society for Accessible Travel & Hospitality (SATH) North America-based travellers. ⓐ 347 5th Avenue, New York, NY 10016, USA ⓣ (212) 447 7284 ⓦ www.sath.org

TOURIST INFORMATION

Kiev has two tourist information offices, and both are a useful source of advice and local information. Many hotels also provide tourist information in English. It is worth contacting a tour operator (see opposite) if you want to make the most of your visit.

Tourist Information Centre 'Kiev' ⓐ Khreschatyk 19A ⓣ 851 8558 ⓛ 10.00–17.00 Mon–Fri, 10.00–14.00 Sat ⓜ Khreschatyk
Kiev Tourist Information Centre ⓐ Kominternu 7/9 ⓣ 490 1711 ⓛ 10.00–19.00 Mon–Fri ⓜ Vokzalna

The following websites contain much useful information about Kiev:

ⓦ www.mfa.gov.ua is the official website of Ukraine's foreign ministry. The English-language 'About Ukraine' section provides consular information and contact details for Ukraine's embassies abroad and foreign embassies in Kiev.

Ⓦ www.kmu.gov.ua is the official web portal of the Ukrainian government.

If you are visiting Lviv or Odessa, check out Ⓦ www.lviv.inyourpocket.com and Ⓦ www.lviv-life.com are useful websites offering information about Lviv in English.
Ⓦ www.odessa.ua is the official website of Odessa's mayor, with an English version giving detailed tourist information.
Ⓦ www.odessaguide.com offers useful information on Odessa in English.
Ⓦ www.odessaapts.com has an online hotel booking service for Odessa.

Tour operators (Ukraine-based tour companies)
Kiev is one of those destinations where even an independent traveller will find that organised sightseeing can be a good way of experiencing a lot in a short time. The following companies are Kiev-based unless otherwise stated:
Mandrivnyk (ⓐ Vorovskoho 22 ⓣ 369 3346 Ⓦ www.mandrivnyk.com.ua) offers cruises, city tours and bus tours through Ukraine. If you can afford it, they can even arrange for a flight in an MiG plane.
Meest-Tour (ⓐ Shevchenka 34, Lviv ⓣ (32) 297 0852 Ⓦ www.meest-tour.com) specialises in adventure tours and hiking trips. It is based in Lviv.
New Logic (see page 112) offers a full range of packages, hotel bookings and theatre tickets. It caters to a younger crowd.
Prime Excursion Bureau (ⓐ Schekavytska 19 ⓣ 227 7778 Ⓦ www.primetour.com.ua) is another reliable option.

Emergencies

EMERGENCY PHONE NUMBERS

Ambulance ⓣ 103

Fire ⓣ 101

Police ⓣ 102

Emergency from any mobile ⓣ 112

MEDICAL EMERGENCIES

Hospitals

Most local hospitals should be avoided if possible. The following are Western-standard hospitals with emergency departments and call centres that are open 24 hours a day:

American Medical Centre ⓐ Berdychivska 1 ⓣ 490 7600 ⓦ www.amcenters.com Metro: Lukyanivska

Boris Clinic ⓐ Chervonoarmiyska (Velyka Vasylkivska) 55A,

EMERGENCY PHRASES

Help! Допоможіть! *Dopomozhit'!*

Call an ambulance/a doctor/the police/the fire brigade!
Викличте швидку допомогу/лікаря/міліцію/пожежних!
Vyklychte shvydku dopomohu/likarya/militsiyu/pozhezhnykh!

Can you help me, please?
Ви не могли б мені допомогти, будь ласка?
Vy ne mogly b meni dopomohty, bud' laska?

at Hotel Sport ⓣ 238 0000 ⓦ www.boris.kiev.ua ⓜ Metro: Respublikansky Stadion

Medikom is Ukraine's first private medical company. ⓐ Kondratyuka 8 ⓣ 503 7777 ⓦ www.medikom.kiev.ua ⓜ Metro: Minska

Pharmacies

Pharmacies are easy to find in Kiev – identifiable by their standard green-and-white colour scheme. The following are open 24 hours:

ⓐ Artema 10 ⓣ 272 1109 ⓜ Metro: Zoloti Vorota

ⓐ Yaroslaviv Val 28 ⓣ 288 0137 ⓜ Metro: Zoloti Vorota

ⓐ Raisy Okipnoyi 4 ⓣ 569 5733 ⓜ Metro: Livoberezhna

ⓐ Chervonoarmiyska (Velyka Vasylkivska) 101 ⓣ 529 1175 ⓜ Metro: Palats "Ukrayina"

POLICE

As fluency in English is not the premium requirement for a career in the police here, it might be easier to report any crimes to your hotel management, or to your tour operator if you are on a package holiday. They can probably help with the proper authorities, and cut through the red tape. But if the crime is serious, go to the police.

EMBASSIES & CONSULATES

Australian Consulate ⓐ Kominternu 18 ⓣ 235 7586 ⓜ Metro: Vokzalna

British Embassy ⓐ Desiatynna 9 ⓣ 490 3660 ⓦ http://ukinukraine.fco.gov.uk ⓜ Metro: Maidan Nezalezhnosti

Canadian Embassy ⓐ Yaroslaviv Val 31 ⓣ 590 3100 ⓦ www.canadainternational.gc.ca ⓜ Metro: Zoloti Vorota

US Embassy ⓐ Yuriya Kotsyubynskoho 10 ⓣ 490 4000 ⓦ http://ukraine.usembassy.gov ⓜ Metro: Lukyanivska

ACKNOWLEDGEMENTS

Thomas Cook Publishing wishes to thank the photographers, picture libraries and other organisations, to whom the copyright belongs, for the photographs in this book.

Artemka/Wikimedia Commons, page 98; BigStockPhoto.com (Natalia Bratslavsky, pages 48 & 55; Yriy Brykaylo, page 125; Maksym Dyachenko, page 19; Valeria Gavrilenko, page 6; Steve Hayes, page 24; Iurii Konoval, page 57; Kashtalian Ludmyla, page 5; Paul Maydikov, pages 8–9; Andrey Nikolajew, page 115; Serge Sapozhnikov, page 39; Valentin Shevchenko, page 142; Sergii Tsololo, pages 41, 64–5 & 74–5); Dreamstime.com (Imyrga, page 59; Natalia Bratslavsky, page 117; Aleksey Kondratyuk, page 133; Iurii Konoval, page 102; Dmitry Naumov, page 35; Photocell, pages 50–51; Volodymyr Romantsov, page 139; Anton Zagorulko, page 107; Yana Zhezhela page 137); iStockphoto.com (Adrian Beesley, pages 128–9; Natalia Bratslavsky, page 10; Oleg Mitiukhin, page 29); layoutcom, page 72; И. Максим, page 92; Tim Judy, page 96; Tony Gervis, pages 20, 23, 27, 32–3, 42, 68, 79, 80, 86, 95, 105, 109 & 113.

Send your thoughts to
books@thomascook.com

- **Found a great bar, club, shop or must-see sight that we don't feature?**
- **Like to tip us off about any information that needs a little updating?**
- **Want to tell us what you love about this handy little guidebook and more importantly how we can make it even handier?**

Then here's your chance to tell all! Send us ideas, discoveries and recommendations today and then look out for your valuable input in the next edition of this title.

Email the above address (stating the title) or write to:
pocket guides Series Editor, Thomas Cook Publishing, PO Box 227, Coningsby Road, Peterborough PE3 8SB, UK.

WHAT'S IN YOUR GUIDEBOOK?

Independent authors Impartial up-to-date information from our travel experts who meticulously source local knowledge.

Experience Thomas Cook's 165 years in the travel industry and guidebook publishing enriches every word with expertise you can trust.

Travel know-how Thomas Cook has thousands of staff working around the globe, all living and breathing travel.

Editors Travel-publishing professionals, pulling everything together to craft a perfect blend of words, pictures, maps and design.

You, the traveller We deliver a practical, no-nonsense approach to information, geared to how you really use it.

For CAMBRIDGE PUBLISHING MANAGEMENT LIMITED:
Project editor: Karen Beaulah
Layout: Paul Queripel
Proofreaders: Ed Robinson & Tom Lee

Useful phrases

English	Ukrainian	*Approx pronunciation*
BASICS		
Yes	Так	*Tak*
No	Ні	*Ni*
Please	Будь ласка	*Bud' laska*
Thank you	Дякую	*Diakuyu*
Hello	Добрий день/Привіт	*Dobryi den'/Pryvit*
Goodbye	До побачення	*Do pobachennia*
Excuse me	Перепрошую	*Pereproshuyu*
Sorry	Вибачте	*Vybachte*
That's okay	Усе гаразд	*Use harazd*
I don't speak Ukrainian	Я не говорю українською	*Ya ne hovoryu ukrayinskoyu*
Do you speak English?	Ви розмовляєте англійською?	*Vy rozmovlyayete anhliys'koyu?*
Good morning	Доброго ранку	*Dobroho ranku*
Good afternoon	Добрий день	*Dobryi den'*
Good evening	Добрий вечір	*Dobryi vechir*
Goodnight	На добраніч	*Na dobranich*
My name is . . .	Мене звуть . . .	*Mene zvut' . . .*
NUMBERS		
One	Один	*Odyn*
Two	Два	*Dva*
Three	Три	*Try*
Four	Чотири	*Chotyry*
Five	П'ять	*P'yat'*
Six	Шість	*Shist'*
Seven	Сім	*Sim*
Eight	Вісім	*Visim*
Nine	Дев'ять	*Devyat'*
Ten	Десять	*Desyat'*
Twenty	Двадцять	*Dvadtsyat'*
Fifty	П'ятдесят	*Pyatdesyat*
One hundred	Сто	*Sto*
SIGNS & NOTICES		
Airport	Аеропорт	*Aeroport*
Railway station	Залізничний вокзал	*Zaliznychnyi vokzal*
Platform	Платформа	*Platforma*
Smoking/ Non-smoking	Місце для паління/ Не палити	*Mistse dlya palinnya/ Ne palyty*
Toilets	Туалети	*Tualety*
Ladies/Gentlemen	Ж (жінки)/Ч (чоловіки)	*Zhinky/Choloviky*
Underground (Subway)	Метро	*Metro*